DAVID CROCKETT WENT DOWN FIGHTING

DAVID CROCKETT WENT DOWN FIGHTING
How We Know It

PHIL GUARNIERI

WITH RICHARD L. RANGE

FOREWORD BY JERRY E. PATTERSON

RED RIVER PRESS
DALLAS, TEXAS

Library of Congress Cataloging-in-Publication Data

Guarnieri, Phil, 1957–
David crockett went down fighting: how we know it/
Phil Guarnieri with Richard L. Range.
I. Range, Richard L., 1952–

Foreword by Jerry E. Patterson

ISBN: 978-0-692-03801-7
1. Crockett, David, 1786–1836. 2. Crockett, Davy, 1786–1836 — Death and burial.
3. Crockett, Davy, 1786–1836 — Legends.
4. Alamo (San Antonio, Tex.) — Battle of the, 1836. 5. Texas — History — Revolution, 1835–1836. 6. Legends — Texas. 7. Unsolved history. 8. Cold case investigation.

Library of Congress Control Number: 2023918093

∞ The paper used in this publication meets the minimum requirements of American National Standard for Information Sciences—Permanence of Paper for Printed Library Materials,
ANSI Z39.48-1992.

Copyright © 2024 by Phil Guarnieri and
Richard L. Range
All rights reserved.

Printed in the United States of America

"A lie can travel halfway around the world before the truth can get its boots on."

—Mark Twain

"A departure from historical truth may be somewhat palliated when intended to cover disgrace; but even then the policy is bad; for such deviations, if touching matters of importance, are in general eventually exposed."

—Reuben Marmaduke Potter

"What happens in the past never really goes away. Maybe time also finds the truth."

—Detective Lilly Rush, character from the dramatic television series *Cold Case*

"I leave this rule for others when I'm dead, Be always sure you're right— THEN GO AHEAD!"

—David Crockett

And perhaps most germane to the subject of this book—both revealing what the man himself was aware of and foreshadowing what in fact has transpired ever since his death:

> "I know not whether, in the eyes of the world,
> a brilliant death is not preferred to
> an obscure life of rectitude.
> Most men are remembered as they died,
> and not as they lived.
> We gaze with admiration upon
> the glories of the setting sun,
> yet scarcely bestow a passing glance
> upon its noonday splendor."
>
> —David Crockett

For My Mother:
Nancy Rose (Leacoma) Guarnieri
An Eternal Inspiration

—Phil Guarnieri

For all the great Texans I have known during my life—so many now sadly passed over to Jordan's other shore. We shall not see your likes again.

—Richard Range

Phil Guarnieri

Phil Guarnieri was born in Gravesend, Brooklyn, New York. He graduated from Saint John's University with a B.A. and M.A. degree in History with a minor in Political Science. At the age of nine years old, he became interested in the story of the Alamo after watching an episode about it on the popular television series *The Time Tunnel*. Ever since then the famous siege and battle has become a lifelong passion. Guarnieri joined the Alamo Society in 1987 and has over the years contributed numerous articles to its quarterly publication, *The Alamo Journal*.

Active in his local community in both civic and political organizations, serving as Chairman and President in several of them, Guarnieri has also served as an elected public official for fifteen years including being a two-term mayor. He was previously an adjunct professor at a Manhattan college where he taught American history, political philosophy, and government.

Guarnieri is also a published author, having written *Inside the Ropes*, the biography of Arthur Mercante, the celebrated professional referee of the greatest prizefights of all time. For several years he wrote numerous articles for *Ring Magazine*, a nationally published sport magazine. Guarnieri is also co-author of the book *Custer's Last Stand Demystified: Story of an Epic Defeat; A Tactical & Timing Analysis of the Little Big*

Horn Battle. In addition, he was a longtime columnist for both local newspapers, the *Gateway Bulletin* and the *Floral Park Dispatch*, with columns respectively titled "Philosophically Speaking" and "Thoughts and Asides."

Guarnieri is currently employed as the Director of Human Resources in the Township of Hempstead, the largest township in the United States. He presently resides in Long Island, New York, with his wife of thirty years, Sonia.

Richard L. Range

Richard L. Range, a fourth-generation Texan, grew up in Irving, Texas, and graduated from West Texas State University in 1974 with a B.M.E. in Education. He taught at the junior high and high school levels before becoming a 31-year career fireman with the Mesquite Fire Department, also serving as Spanish translator for both the fire and police departments. He has been a longtime collector and shooter of black-powder small arms and has attended gunnery school for muzzleloading artillery.

Richard Range previously served as a board member of the Alamo Society, an international association of Alamo authors, scholars, researchers, and dedicated enthusiasts. Over the years he has published numerous articles in the quarterly publication of the Alamo Society, *The Alamo Journal*. Range has also given several presentations on the Alamo at the annual Alamo Society Symposium. These presentations have dealt with the physical structures and defensive fortification features of the Alamo extant in 1836, the specific artillery pieces present for the Alamo's defense including the history of where each of those barrels came from and where they are located today, programs on his conclusions concerning the troop numbers and casualties incurred by both sides at the Alamo battle, and the sequential details of the battle itself.

Also a member of the Alamo Battlefield Association, the San Jacinto Battleground Conservancy, and an associate member of the Alamo Defenders Descendants Association, Range has spent over twenty years in Alamo research in both English and Spanish. For this book he has retranslated virtually all of the quoted materials and primary source documents from the original Spanish into English.

In addition, over the last thirty-five years Range has worked as a practicing paralegal, during which time he has researched, drafted, and written numerous legal briefs and otherwise participated in many cases at trial, from the District Court level up to the Supreme Court of Texas.

DEDICATION

This book is dedicated to the memory of
all the courageous Heroes of the Alamo.
The people of Texas are forever in their debt.

"Texas, O Texas! Your freeborn single star,
Sends out its radiance to nations near and far.
Emblem of freedom! It sets our hearts aglow,
With thoughts of San Jacinto and glorious Alamo."

—Excerpt from the official State Song
"Texas, Our Texas"

"It is foolish and wrong to mourn the men who died.
Rather, we should thank God that such men lived."

—General George S. Patton

FOREWORD

"Davy, Davy Crockett, King of the Wild Frontier"

If you were born in the 1940's or early 50's I'm sure you recognize the lyric above. An entire generation of boys and girls sat in front of black and white television sets on Sunday evenings watching Walt Disney himself introduce the latest episode of *The Adventures of Davy Crockett*—with "The Ballad of Davy Crockett" as the introduction soundtrack.

I was one of them, and yes, I had a coonskin cap and a toy rifle that looked to me exactly like Davy's.

The Alamo show premiered on February 23, 1955 and I'm willing to bet I was in the audience—I've checked out that episode on YouTube and yes, I remember it.

Disney's "Davy Crockett at the Alamo" episode provided no answer to the question "how did Davy die?" Of course one wouldn't expect a 1950's TV show to provide such an answer. In fact, Davy didn't even die in the final minute of the Alamo episode. The last we saw of him he was swinging his rifle at the enemy and we were left hanging as to the final result.

Nonetheless, we were sure, along with the rest of Texas and Texans, that Davy Crockett had fought until his last breath and he was the ultimate Texas hero.

Ironically in the same year that the Disney Davy died at the TV Alamo, the diary of a Mexican officer present at the Alamo, José Enrique de la Peña, surfaced and suggested that Davy Crockett had surrendered.

The diary's authenticity was subject to question—and parts of it still are—but de la Peña's surrender version gained traction and eventually became mainstream. About the time *Texas Monthly*'s November 1986 version told us that Crockett surrendered, academia had wholly embraced the same conclusion.

What if he surrendered, or was captured, or whatever? Is surrendering with the possibility you might live to fight another day an ignoble choice? Even if executed, wasn't that end still giving your life for your country?

About thirty years ago I concluded that Crockett surrendered or was captured and executed. It didn't make any difference to me. He still died nobly. He was still a hero.

Now I've changed my mind. Crockett died fighting. Am I 100 percent sure? No, but at my age I've learned that 100 percent sure is always a bad place to be.

You've read this far, so obviously you've got the narrative in hand. Don't stop now. Read on. This relatively short but well-documented treatise is definitely worth your time.

If you believe Crockett surrendered, I promise you will at least have very serious doubts about the surrender narrative, and more likely conclude as I did, "I was wrong, he died fighting"—no matter what de la Peña wrote.

Remember the Alamo.

Jerry E. Patterson
Former Texas State Senator
Former Texas General Land Office Commissioner
Lt. Col. USMCR, Ret.

PREFACE

by Richard L. Range

"Facts are stubborn things; and whatever may be our wishes, our inclinations, or the dictates of our passions, they cannot alter the state of facts and evidence."

—John Adams

The authors wish to make completely clear up front what the goal of this book is and what it is not. Unlike much of the previous argumentation regarding the controversy of whether David Crockett died fighting or was captured and executed, this book is not concerned with either of the following issues:
1. The validation and perpetuation (nor the disproval) of any "legend" or "mythology" concerning the person of David Crockett.
2. Any issue or factor involving race whatsoever. There were, after all, Mexican participants on both sides in the battle of the Alamo. It is also now known that there were a number of African-American combatants, both slave and free, among the Alamo defenders as well. Regardless of ethnic background, all of the

defenders were united in the effort to resist and oppose, to the death if necessary, the tyrannical rule of a dictator.

Although often inserted into the debate by proponents of Crockett's execution, neither one of the prior matters has anything at all to do with the question of whether the execution story is correct.

What *is* the goal and total focus of this book is to determine if in fact there is a valid, supportable way to ascertain the true circumstances of the death of David Crockett—an issue that in actuality has been in question ever since the battle on March 6, 1836.

In pursuit of that objective, the authors have performed a comprehensive forensic analysis employing the accepted and acknowledged intellectual process of seeking the truth by means of inference from the known facts, the extant evidence, and the application of sound logic and reason—the same investigative techniques that have been used to solve large numbers of cold-case murders and other crimes. We have utilized this method, with no preconceived notions or preferred outcome, in an earnest effort to reach a reliable conclusion that is supported by at least a preponderance of the evidence, and, ideally, beyond a reasonable doubt. By introducing two new pieces of previously unrecognized crucial evidence that have never been raised or even considered throughout the entire course of this controversy, we believe that we have succeeded in our endeavor to finally uncover the truth surrounding Crockett's death.

It is of course up to each reader to conclude whether we have achieved that goal. Either way, and however he died, David Crockett without a doubt died a hero, as did all the rest of the defenders at the Alamo—just by being there.

ACKNOWLEDGMENTS

The authors wish to thank a number of people who generously gave of their time and effort to read the manuscript and provide helpful suggestions. These include Raymond Cruz, Charles Goolsby, Brad Ponder, James Donovan, Craig Covner, Russ Foster, Gary Wiggins, and Tom Feely. Noted author and historian Gregg Dimmick graciously furnished insightful advice that led to multiple revisions and improvements to the manuscript as it was being developed.

We especially want to acknowledge Pat Haddock who spent literally hundreds of hours assisting with the research, editing, and formatting of the book, Catherine Baker who is responsible for the book's layout and design, and Ann Levin for her help in the publication of the book.

And lastly, the authors wish to express our sincere appreciation to Jerry Patterson for all of his decades of dedicated service to the State of Texas and for writing the Foreword to this book.

DAVID CROCKETT WENT DOWN FIGHTING

PROLOGUE

by Phil Guarnieri

"In war, the first casualty is truth."

—Aeschylus, Greek tragic dramatist,
525 B.C.–456 B.C.

Ever since the ancient Greeks, much of the writing of history has been shaped more by lies, half-truths, and innuendo than by facts. Such is the case with the fireball of controversy that ignited around the controversial death of David Crockett. Though a minor subject against the vast and daunting backdrop of the past, this nearly 200-year mystery has engendered a disproportionate and consuming interest relative to its historical importance. This is because the Alamo, like Crockett himself, is an outsized story and speaks to our deepest ideals about the meaning of courage, patriotism, and sacrifice.

This small work is dedicated to answering one large and consuming question: Is there a reliable and credible means to determine the actual manner of David Crockett's death—a subject in dispute since the very day the famous battle took place. The authors strongly believe that when viewed as a whole, the evidence convincingly weighs in favor of the conclusion that the famous frontiersman was slain sometime during the battle and was not one of the handful of prisoners that Santa Anna ordered executed in its aftermath. It might sound audacious to say, but we think we can prove it.

The authors agree with the prevailing opinion that whatever the circumstances of Crockett's death at the Alamo, what matters most is that he insisted on and fought for a Republic—an idea he treasured and for which he ultimately gave his life. But that is almost beside the point of this book insofar as it makes not a particle of difference in solving the mystery of his death one way or the other.

Even though this debate has spanned nearly a half-century, when rereading the accounts purporting Crockett's execution, we were surprised how they read more like a parade of anecdotes than a set of facts. Yet it was these same accounts that once provided the fodder for many writers, academicians, and opinion makers to engage in another fashionable denigration of an American hero celebrated in books, cinema, and popular culture. Iconoclasm has always had a sporting and fetching quality about it and more than a few relished the opportunity to depict the "King of the Wild Frontier" groveling before his captors.

For those weaned on Disney's Crockett and proud Texans in general, the world was turned upside down although the execution story is as old as the battle itself. All this tumult began innocently enough when Carmen Perry, a native of Mexico, and Director of the Daughters of the Republic of Texas Library, completed an English translation of an account relating to the fall of the Alamo written by an intelligent Mexican officer named José Enrique de la Peña. Peña claimed to have been an eyewitness to Crockett's execution and recounted its epic drama in searing and memorable prose. The publication in 1975 of Perry's translation, *With Santa Anna in Texas: A Personal Narrative of the Revolution*, with the unsuspected Crockett paragraph buried between its covers like a hidden land mine, caused an explosion that would not only rock Texas but send ripples of shock waves reaching all those who cherished the story of the Alamo.

As the controversy heated up, combusting into a five-alarm conflagration, an enterprising Texan named Dan Kilgore, an accountant and President of the Texas State Historical Association, saw commercial potential in all the public wrangling and in 1978 would argue in book form that Peña's account and other lesser supporting documents were reliable and that the Crockett hero-worshippers should wipe the slate clean of their indelible and cherished childhood memories of Walt Disney showing Davy swinging Old Betsy against hordes of Mexican soldiers in a last-ditch defense within the crumbling walls of the Alamo.

Disney's dramatic 1955 climax had precipitated a cultural and commercial phenomenon of everything Davy Crockett, making the closing fade-out of a generational icon going down fighting an idée fixe in the minds of millions of Baby Boomers at an impressionable age. Undermining this image of a near godlike figure risked public outrage, and that is exactly what Kilgore triggered in publishing his own monograph with the pithy title, *How Did Davy Die?* In his short discourse, Kilgore compiled every scrap of evidence and used every slant imaginable to prove his thesis that Crockett did not die on the besieged and bloody ramparts of the Alamo but was indeed taken prisoner and executed.

The avalanche of scorn was now redirected toward Kilgore who, though forewarned, at least professed to have been totally unsuspecting of the quite predictable scathing backlash. Trapped in a cauldron of unremitting invective, he behaved more honorably than many of his critics who resorted to slanderous attacks on his character accusing him, among other things, of being a closet Communist. The hysterical and self-conscious partisanship this little book generated created an unhealthy state of affairs, crippling honest debate, poisoning civil discourse, and bringing us further from the truth.

Although we sympathize with the crucible Kilgore endured, we believe that *How Did Davy Die?* is badly and even fatally scarred by the author's own preconceptions, omissions, and logical inconsistencies.

As just one example of his many misconceptions and factual errors, Kilgore has two of the key Texan eyewitnesses who identified Crockett's dead body, Susannah Dickinson and Travis's slave Joe, as being captured in the same place, at the same time, and by the same English-speaking Mexican officer—all of which are verifiably incorrect. (Dickinson was sequestered in the Sacristy, a room inside the back of the Alamo Church; Joe had retreated to Travis's headquarters, the Treviño house, located on the West Wall on the completely opposite side of the Alamo compound. Dickinson, as will be demonstrated later in this book, had already been escorted out of the Alamo by the time Joe was discovered. And Dickinson was rescued by Colonel Juan Almonte, while Joe was saved by Captain Barragán—two entirely different English-speaking Mexican officers.)

Another factual error (or blatant falsehood) was Kilgore's statement that "not one report of an eyewitness has been found by Alamo scholars to support the popular notion that Crockett went down while desperately clubbing Mexican soldiers with the barrel of his shattered rifle"—completely ignoring three such accounts given independently by members of the Mexican attack force at the Alamo, two captains and one sergeant, who all described David Crockett's death in exactly that manner. (Intriguingly, these soldiers also described accurately and in detail the appearance of his peculiar clothing and cap, as well as making the same specific statement that Crockett sustained a gunshot that broke his *right* arm prior to being killed).

Possibly worse still, in his book Kilgore was guilty of giving quotations that were incomplete, allowing him the opportunity of mischaracterizing what the sources actually stated, when the full quotes would have weakened his arguments. A case in point—Kilgore cited newspaper accounts that began circulating not long after the battle describing David Crockett as being among a group of defenders who had tried to surrender and asked for quarter. Upon being refused they continued fighting until all were butchered. Kilgore quoted the first part about Crockett having been one of the men who "had tried to surrender," but completely omitted the later part about "continued fighting until all were butchered." By this omission, he implied that these various articles constituted early evidence of David Crockett's *capture and execution*—which they clearly were not.

And then there is perhaps Kilgore's most egregious and glaring logical inconsistency—after listing and describing several Mexican accounts of Crockett being captured and executed and concluding that many of them were highly questionable at best if not outright fantastical, admitting that "any one of them, standing alone, could be subject to question," he nevertheless then proceeded to count *all* of them in his tally anyway, claiming that in total they comprised "*a massive body of evidence*" for Crockett's execution. Kilgore not so much ended a myth as created one of his own. We hope to set the record straight with a more discriminating and evenhanded approach.

The whole saga of David Crockett's death is indeed interesting and complicated, and much of the dissent against the conventional wisdom that Crockett was executed has already been related by others including several efforts by Bill Groneman, William C. Davis in an article entitled "How Davy Probably Didn't Die"—a play on words of Kilgore's book, and in the exhaustive endnotes of James Donovan's critically acclaimed *The Blood of Heroes* in which he persuasively argued that David Crockett most likely was not executed. There is an element of truth in Cormac McCarthy's observation that "books are made out of books" and we have written this one because we believe there is something old to affirm and something new to say. Granting this we gratefully acknowledge the contributions of our predecessors and hope to do them justice by advancing and building upon what they have so ably laid out.

This brings us to our own concise volume in which we seek to reach a reliable conclusion as to the actual manner of Crockett's death. We realize that no one can either write, or live for that matter, without preconceptions and we are no exception. But it is not our own frailties that we ask to be judged, but rather the evidence presented. It is these grounds alone that will either sustain or topple our arguments.

By presenting *two new elements* of critical evidence that have not ever been examined at any point in the whole duration of this raucous and never-ending debate, we trust that we have accomplished our objective to at last ascertain the true circumstances of Crockett's death.

Long after we are gone the historical record will endure. We sincerely hope that our efforts have served a constructive role in ensuring that record to be accurate with respect to David Crockett's ultimate fate at the Alamo.

David Crockett: Man and Myth
Backwoodsman, Politician, American Folk Hero

The eventful and extraordinary life of David Crockett began in East Tennessee on August 17, 1786, in what is today Greene County. Nurtured and suckled in America's backwoods he would earn a legendary reputation for hunting and storytelling. Both skills would later fuel the start of his rambunctious political career. It would not be an exaggeration to say that he was the mightiest hunter in the West, regularly providing meat not only for his own growing household but, in the spirit of frontier generosity, for his neighbors in times of scarcity. One marker of his hunting prowess and his proficiency with the long rifle came in 1826, perhaps abetted by a number of earthquakes that had dislodged hibernating bears in the Mississippi region, when he killed 105 bears in the span of less than a year, forty-seven in one particularly miraculous month, and six deer in one day.

While Crockett was always more of a woodsman than a warrior, he had also come to know war in a very intimate way. Crockett participated in the hard fighting during the Creek Indian war under the command of the nation's future president, Major General Andrew Jackson. During this campaign, a searing and haunting experience was burned into Crockett's memory. On August 30, 1813, the Creeks surprised the garrison at Fort Mims in Alabama slaughtering more than 500 soldiers and settlers, regardless of sex and age, in the most horrific and depraved manner. In reprisal, on November 3, 1813, the American army attacked a Creek Indian village at Tallusahatchee and massacred nearly 200 inhabitants—not only warriors but also women and children. The brutal and savage attack made a deep and enduring impression on the 27-year-old Crockett teaching him about the merciless wages of frontier warfare.

Crockett returned home after his 3-month enlistment was up, but he re-enlisted as a sergeant in September of 1814 to drive the British and their allies out of the territories of the United States. They spent several arduous months chasing Indians through the swamps and forests of Florida and Alabama while suffering from low rations, exposure, and the unforgiving elements that continually assailed them. With his marvelous hunting skills, despite the scarcity of large game, Crockett helped ease his outfit's dire hunger by killing whatever small game was available. But this only delayed the inevitable. While the men survived, their horses finally gave out and Crockett left before his enlistment expired. But he had, said author James Donovan, gained more than enough experience of soldiering.

Back at home and hearth Crockett's ambitions turned in another direction. His barnstorming hyperbolic tales, congenial disposition, and rustic simplicity made him a natural for local politics. With his trusty long rifle, which he affectionately named Old Betsy, the man and his weapon pole-vaulted into American mythology. This reputation served him well, and in 1817 Crockett was appointed magistrate, then justice of the peace, and in 1818 a town commissioner of Lawrenceburg and also elected a colonel in the Tennessee Militia.

After resigning those posts, in 1821 and 1823 he twice won a seat in the Tennessee General Assembly, first representing a district in Middle Tennessee and the second time representing a district in West Tennessee. In 1825 Crockett made a failed first bid for the United States House of Representatives from West Tennessee, but in 1827 was successfully elected and re-elected in 1829. He lost the seat in 1831 only to regain it in 1833.

His ruggedness, triumphs of endurance, and sheer stamina made him stand out from all the other tall-tale tellers and raconteurs. Crockett possessed qualities, his principal biographer James Shackford noted, that made people notice and talk about him. No matter how extravagant the telling—like bestriding a tornado or whipping his weight in wildcats—it was never entirely absent of credibility because of what they knew him to be in real life. Those hardy and heroic qualities of the frontier were made manifest in his person and his feats were well known among his peers: His unusual determination to cross a swollen river in midwinter to get to his keg of powder, pursuing a grizzly all night alone and not turning back until he bagged his prey, setting out as a 12-year-old trudging miles through the deep snow in order to escape from his roguish employer and, of course, his nonpareil marksmanship and hunting skills. This was the stuff of myth, and if there are urban legends that are spoken of today, there were also backwoods legends of yesteryear, and David Crockett, along with Daniel Boone, was at its apogee.

The blade of growing fame was further honed when he wrote down his own story publishing it under the title *A Narrative of the Life of David Crockett of the State of Tennessee.* Based more on fact than invention, the book became an instant bestseller when it hit the market in the spring of 1834. It turned out the real-life David gave the fictional Davy the stamp of authenticity. As Shackford reminds us, the qualities of uncommon strength, unusual perseverance, extraordinary courage, and unbelievable determination were the measures of a man because they were, in a very real sense, the measures of life in the world that Crockett lived in.

But while his fame grew there were dark clouds on the horizon. For as suited as he was in some ways for the political arena, he was sorely lacking in others. His gift for humor, communicable likability, and hardscrabble background won him popularity—but he also lacked perspective and political adeptness. Eventually his stubbornness and inability to compromise took their toll.

Crockett's tall tales would lose their luster among Washington's power circle, and he would run afoul of his former military commander, President Andrew Jackson, partly over Jackson's Indian Removal Act of 1830—a measure that Crockett had opposed—but mostly because of Crockett's staunch support of squatters' rights for the pioneering homesteaders as opposed to the interests of the wealthy planters and moneyed land speculators who were financially supporting Jackson—a stance that earned Crockett the reputation as a champion of the common man.

Crockett openly and publicly defied Jackson, boasting that he would never wear a collar labeled "MY DOG" in submission to "Old Hickory." He accused the President of being a greater tyrant than Cromwell, Caesar, and Bonaparte. By now Jackson had finally had enough of this bumptious bumpkin and turned the full weight of his considerable political power against Crockett to drive him out of office once and for all.

In the ensuing, rancorous electoral contest on August 6, 1835, he lost by the slim margin of 252 votes out of 9,052 cast. Now abandoned by the Whigs who had been using the former Democrat for their own advantage, Crockett was down but not defeated. On October 31, 1835, his old optimism resurfaced, and he wrote to his brother-in-law that he was headed to the promised land of Texas. It would be one last adventure to explore the wild that he so passionately thrived in. Even during Crockett's years in elected office where he stepped away from his buckskin and coonskin cap demeanor to cultivate a quasi-gentlemanly appearance, the backwoods never left him, and he frequently went on long hunts that proved for him a tonic as he luxuriated in the company of good and faithful companions, reveling in the manly joy of testing himself in the barrens and wilderness. It was as inseparable from Crockett as his heartbeat was from his heart.

With his political career in tatters, Crockett, in his frank and colorful way of speaking, told his constituents that he had done his best for them, but since they did not return him to office, they could "all go to Hell"—he would "Go to Texas." On November 1, 1835, Crockett mounted a large bay horse and before family and friends took the first step on that fateful journey. He set out with his nephew and two other men. Others would accompany them for a time and later leave throughout the route to and through Texas. In the end, only Crockett and his nephew would still be together when they finally arrived and enlisted at Nacogdoches in January of 1836. (The nephew, William Patton, did not fight and die at the Alamo but did later fight at the Battle of San Jacinto.)

There are those who have adopted the preposterous notion that at age 49, Crockett was an old man. Nothing could be further from the truth. Born with an amazingly stout and robust constitution, fortified and tempered by an almost unimaginably taxing and Spartan lifestyle, the vigorous outdoor life had toughened and hardened him in ways almost unimaginable to our modern and cushioned way of life.

The itinerary that Crockett undertook on horseback is a testament to his strength, resilience, and tenacity. As he journeyed with a few companions to his ultimate destination in San Antonio, of the hundreds who saw him and heard him speak there is not a single reference of anyone recording any signs of frailty, age, or infirmity right up to when he lost his life at the Alamo more than four months later. Only a strong and hardy soul could have withstood the challenges of such a journey.

Setting off on their trek, Crockett's small company proceeded down the Mississippi River to Memphis. There they crossed the Mississippi and traveled on to Little Rock, from Little Rock to Fulton and Lost Prairie in southwestern Arkansas, then westward up the Red

River. Their exact route thereafter is uncertain, but they most likely crossed the Red River into Texas north of Clarksville, turned west at Clarksville, and headed through Honey Grove and Fannin County—the place where Crockett wrote that he had found his dreamt-of piece of Texas on which he intended to later homestead.

Crockett and his band reportedly continued westward hunting buffalo, reaching as far as the headwaters of the East Fork of the Trinity River about 55 miles to the north of Dallas, where they finally circled back eastward past Clarksville and then eventually set out south for Nacogdoches which they reached in early January of 1836. From there he traveled to San Augustine, back to Nacogdoches, then later going to Washington-on-the-Brazos and on to San Antonio.

During this 14-week excursion, Crockett had sometimes slogged miles in the rain and biting wind, through mud, streams, over hills and rugged country, crossing mighty rivers in frigid climes while mostly hunting for his food and, when he could not find even rough shelter along the way, making the very earth his bed and the starry skies his roof.

Despite this monumental journey totaling over 1,200 miles, Crockett showed no fatigue. He was a magnet for attention and wherever there was a crowd to be had, he speechified with vigor whether he was in Memphis, where he gave his "go to hell—I'm going to Texas" speech, a line that always got a big, cheering reaction if not a standing ovation—or whether on a flatboat below the Union Hotel or on a steamboat along the Mississippi where he backslapped and rubbed elbows, swapped jokes and stories in what was an unrelenting parade of conviviality and all-night get-togethers. Wherever Crockett went he found himself in the limelight—banquets were thrown in his honor, a cannon blast saluted his arrival at Nacogdoches and at San Augustine, and in another town he was treated to a fife and drum rendition of "Hail the Conquering Hero."

Throughout Crockett gave every indication of a man in the prime of life. He was always the dynamo exuding vitality and verve. When a committee of Little Rock citizens went to greet him, they found him not at rest from his journey but skinning a deer in the backyard of the Jeffries Hotel in what was another prized kill for this fabled hunter. Like another legendary woodsman, Daniel Boone, Crockett defied aging and fatigue. After one long hunt in Boone's twilight years, his much younger companions were astonished at how he had managed to stand up as well as they had. Boone was 73 years old at the time.

There is another side of Crockett that was just as impressive. He may not have been the most calculating and judicious politician, but he was a man of unwavering principle, ready and willing to stand up for what he believed in. "Be always sure you're right—then go ahead," he was fond of saying and it became his cachet. Once he set on his course nothing, neither man nor beast, could deter him whether it was chasing a bear for miles over severe and laborious terrain, or standing up against the formidable Andrew Jackson—the most powerful man in the United States—or, as it would turn out, facing down Santa Anna's army.

By the time Crockett crossed the Red River into Texas, an armed revolution was already underway. Texas was in critical need of able-bodied men for the defense of the budding nation. Crockett fit the bill, and instead of heading down to the Rio Grande as he originally intended, the fateful decision would be made to go and defend a once broken-down mission now turned into a fortress of sorts called the Alamo. He was all too willing to do his part in the fight, but when Justice John Forbes had earlier administered the oath of allegiance, Crockett could not help but notice that the language required him to uphold any future government. No sir. Crockett insisted that the wording in his oath be changed to a more ringing and idealistic "any future *republican* government," an amendment that the judge was happily obliged to make. Crockett's father and uncle had fought in the American Revolution to rid the colonies of the King. He would not tolerate any kind of despotism or dictatorship, robbing the common folks of this land of their God-given rights.

When Crockett arrived in San Antonio de Béxar on or around February 8, he was greeted with the usual exuberant fanfare. His speech was poignant, inclusive, and humbly delivered ending with:

> And fellow citizens, I am among you. I have come to your country, though not, I hope, through any selfish motive whatever. I have come to aid you all that I can in your noble cause. I shall identify myself with your interests, and all the honor that I desire is that of defending as a high Private, in common with my fellow-citizens, the liberties of our common country.

Doctor John Sutherland, Alamo defender and courier, would later note that this speech made many a man who had not known him before Colonel Crockett's friend. Some two weeks later the Mexican army stunned the Texans by arriving in Béxar much earlier than expected which then drove the defenders into the Alamo. Despite that just 800 yards away, a blood red flag waved menacingly high atop the San Fernando Church tower signifying no quarter, no mercy; despite Santa Anna's ultimatum to surrender or the garrison would be put to the sword; despite being outnumbered ten to one, Crockett told Alamo Commander William Barret Travis, "Colonel, here am I. Assign me a position, and I and my twelve boys will try and defend it."

Travis assigned Crockett and his companions, now proudly called the Tennessee Mounted Volunteers, to what was considered to be the most vulnerable defensive point in the mission—a 115-foot-long rough log palisade consisting of vertical cedar posts reaching perhaps 7 feet high from ground level that ran diagonally from the Church to the low barracks on the south side of the Alamo compound. It was the toughest assignment in the fort.

Having decided on the rightness of the cause and his course, no matter the odds against him, no matter the prospect of a violent death, David Crockett followed his conviction and his motto, and he would "Go ahead" to his death and immortality.

David Crockett Went Down Fighting:
How We Know It

"Just because someone says something is true does not mean that it is."
—Plato

"Rumors are hearsay; they are told, believed, and passed on not because of the weight of evidence but because of the expectations by tellers that they are true in the first place."
—Erich Goode & Nachman Ben-Yehuda

"The most effective way to destroy a people is to deny and obliterate their own understanding of their history."
—George Orwell

With the media splash given to the 2021 iconoclastic book *Forget the Alamo* by three authors betrothed to the emergent woke politics and its evangelical zeal to cashier and desecrate anything that was touched, even tangentially, by slavery, the foundation story of Texas and its historical narrative, so deeply embedded and venerated in the American consciousness, is in jeopardy of being expunged as nothing more than an agenda to celebrate white supremacy.

As a general proposition, these authors' arguments are hopelessly mired in error, bereft of context, and largely anti-historical. Exhorting us to forget a saga that should not only be remembered but richly deserves an outsized place in the national memory is ultimately self-defeating. Even stripped of its embellishments, the epic struggle at the Alamo remains as extraordinary a testament of courage and sacrifice that our nation has to offer, and memories of its martyrdom can only be erased at our own peril.

When Colonel William Barret Travis penned the immortal lines, ". . . I am determined to sustain myself as long as possible & die like a soldier who never forgets what is due to his own honor & that of his country," those words could have been written by any one of the approximately two hundred garrison members who endured thirteen days of siege by an army that outnumbered them twelve to one.

As to the larger issues of the Texas Revolution that are now being pilloried by the politically motivated, these are not the only targets they have taken aim at. Not content to just savage the moral underpinnings of the Texas Revolution, the "Forget the Alamo" contingent, as a kind of coup de grâce, contemptuously gives the boot to such legends as Travis drawing the line in the sand and Davy Crockett going down swinging Old Betsy. And yet there may be more of the truth than the lie in those tales.

Travis's Line in the Sand

As for Travis's drawing of the line, there is more reason than ever to believe it just might have happened. Although some have yet to wholeheartedly subscribe to it (even though every day of the siege the garrison remained defiant, they were crossing a line of their own choosing) over the years the evidence has grown stronger not weaker for it.

From the time in 1873 when Texas Revolution veteran and historian William P. Zuber told the story of a Louis "Moses" Rose showing up at his parents' doorstep in 1836 to relate the extraordinary tale of how he alone had refused to cross Travis's line to fight to the death—to when Texas researcher and County Clerk Robert B. Blake, in the year 1939, uncovered evidence in the Nacogdoches County Courthouse convincingly showing that there had been a Louis Rose in the Alamo and that his testimony was, without exception, accepted by the Local Board of Land Commissioners on behalf of multiple members of the Alamo garrison killed there—to Walter Lord's celebrated book *A Time to Stand* in which he presents a formal statement given by Alamo survivor Susannah Dickinson to the State Adjutant General in 1877 regarding her account of the line—to James Donovan in his well-received book *The Blood of Heroes* who uncovered fresh evidence from several reliable sources, including a clergyman known for his truthfulness, that Susannah Dickinson had told them about the line years before Zuber first published his story of Travis's shatteringly heroic gesture in the last desperate days of the siege—the story has gained a measure of credence and the reader is encouraged to consult these sources for himself.

David Crockett's Death:
The Genesis and Accounts Behind the Controversy

This analysis however is confined to the controversial death of David Crockett and why, when reviewed as a whole, the evidence argues convincingly that the famous frontiersman was not one of the prisoners executed by the order of General Antonio López de Santa Anna after the battle.

Ever since that fateful, cruel, and bloody morning when Santa Anna commanded some five to seven prisoners, the figures vary, to be murdered in cold blood, the gnawing and contentious question is not whether this event occurred—most historians believe it did, as do we—but whether Crockett was among those executed, or was his name inserted for dramatic effect because of his great fame and because he would be a lightning rod for those in the Mexican army who bitterly hated Santa Anna and wanted to blame him for the ruined and ignominious Texas campaign—not to mention the multitude of Texans and other Americans who were also clamoring for the dictator's death.

In order to establish perspective and a timeline, we first must review the genesis of the execution story and see how it unfolded as it did.

March 11, 1836

Information first surfaced about the Alamo executions on March 11, 1836, just five days after the fort fell to the Mexican army. The news was initially brought to the town of Gonzales by Andrés Barcenas and Anselmo Vergara, two residents of San Antonio de Béxar. Neither was an eyewitness to the battle, but Vergara brought information from one Antonio Pérez who had gone to San Antonio and had been told about the battle from an individual whose identity has come down to us only as "D."

This "D" stated that his family lived near the Alamo and that he witnessed the battle from his home. At first he offered scant details, but later he said:

- Travis committed suicide (untrue).
- Bowie was killed in his sickbed (true).
- Almeron Dickinson died when he was shot off the wall while trying to escape with his child in his arms (partially true—the victim was not Dickinson but probably Anthony Wolfe, who had two younger boys ensconced in the fortification).
- And that members of the garrison had been executed after the battle (also true), but he furnished no names.

This was the information that General Sam Houston, Commander-in-Chief of Texas's flailing army, heard early on about the executions but details about the Alamo, other than it fell, seemed to interest him very little. Even when Santa Anna became General Houston's prisoner following the dictator's defeat at San Jacinto, Houston never questions him about the war crime of executing the Alamo prisoners and inquires nothing about the Alamo's trinity of heroes Travis, Bowie, and of course, Crockett. We could speculate here on reasons why (and a couple do come to mind), but this is not necessarily germane to the issue at hand.

March 28, 1836

Within just a few weeks, news concerning the circumstances surrounding the deaths of certain defenders, especially those of the Alamo leaders, began to appear and circulate in various newspapers and personal letters, several including purported accounts of David Crockett's demise. On March 28, the *New-Orleans Commercial Bulletin* carried the story of William Travis and James Bowie committing suicide and seven members of the garrison attempting to surrender, were denied, and then resumed fighting until they were killed, but there is no mention of David Crockett as being among them.

Meanwhile, a letter written by Andrew Briscoe on March 11 (one of the earliest accounts) printed in both the Natchitoches, Louisiana *Red River Herald* and the New Orleans *Louisiana Advertiser* on March 28 states Crockett died fighting like a tiger. Yet, strangely enough, in this same periodical, from a report of unstated origin, another story surfaced that Crockett, James Bonham, and Jesse Benton (who was not even in the Alamo) had asked for quarter and when refused fought to the death.

An identical story appeared in the *New Orleans Post and Union*, spread through the American press, and found its way into Mary Austin Holley's 1836 guidebook, *Texas*, published later that year in which she would include Crockett's death in combat after attempting to surrender. Putting the story in book form, says the historian William C. Davis, author of the critically acclaimed *Three Roads to the Alamo*, helped give credence to what Davis says was clearly still a rumor.

April 1, 1836

This narrative picked up steam on April 1 when the *Mississippi Free Trader and Natchez Gazette* published a March 16 letter from Washington-on-the-Brazos by Charles B. Stewart who melodramatically wrote how all but seven were killed and that "these called for Santa Anna and quarter, and were by *his* order immediately sacrificed." Stewart makes no mention of Crockett however. A week later the same paper repeated much of this story, but this time colored it with stories from passengers who had arrived in New Orleans from Texas on the steamship *Comanche*—again news that Travis and Bowie committed suicide, but also added that Crockett along with others tried to surrender but were killed fighting.

It is William Davis's plausible contention that the information circle regarding the deaths of certain defenders began with Barcenas and Vergara, then went to General Houston, through the American press to New Orleans, to Mexico, and back north to the Mexican prisoners held at Galveston after the Battle of San Jacinto where these camps, as San Jacinto veteran William Zuber noted, became factories for lurid, unsubstantiated rumors, most popular of which were the circumstances surrounding Crockett's death.

Todd Hansen, author of the masterful *The Alamo Reader* (a comprehensive compilation of and analysis and commentary on the primary and secondary sources, accounts, and documents regarding the Alamo), concurred with Davis stating that the Crockett attribution as being among the group that attempted to surrender was seeded in the Little Rock *Arkansas Gazette* on April 12 as a distortion of the original story published in the *New-Orleans Commercial Bulletin* on March 28. A sort of 19th-century telephone game was at work—where one telling embellishes upon the prior one although these stories were second- and thirdhand accounts.

Following April 1836

In the weeks and months following April (and, significantly, after their resounding defeat at San Jacinto on April 21st), a number of accounts by members of the Mexican military regarding Crockett's capture *and execution* first began to appear, with some of them not coming to light until years or even several decades later. A few were published in the newspapers at the time, soon faded from public consciousness, and were not finally rediscovered by historians until well over a century later in the 1960's. (Expert authority Todd Hansen made the very telling point that "not one of the Crockett execution sources is truly confirmed as being attributable *prior* to San Jacinto." And as other researchers on this subject have previously noted, many of the Mexican prisoners from the San Jacinto battle—and later the Mexican veterans who stayed in Texas after the war—were apparently more than willing to tell the Texans anything that they thought the victors might like to hear, especially something denigrating to Santa Anna.)

Some of these Mexican accounts were dishwater weak, the Lieutenant Colonel Fernando Urriza account—the first known version by a *named, identified* participant to be published in permanent form appearing twenty-three years after David Crockett's death in the 1859 *Texas Almanac*—for example talking about atrocities committed against a stooped-over "old man" he *believed they called* "Coket" (and describes him as the only man executed).

Likewise in the same vein, the Captain José Juan Sánchez-Navarro account stating that "Some cruelties horrified me, among others the death of an 'old man' named 'Cocran' and of a young boy about fourteen years old." Again, by all accounts, David Crockett (quite vigorous and not yet fifty years of age) did not have the appearance of an "old man"—stooped-over or otherwise. There was another Alamo defender named Cochran (Robert E. Cochran), but this man was only twenty-six years old.

There is a third account by a Mexican sergeant even weaker than the first two (in fact, outright absurd), claiming that Travis was found sitting on the floor of a room together with Crockett, and that they then attempted to buy their way out of the situation by presenting a roll of bank bills before they were both taken out and executed. In later years, this sergeant did admit that he was not really sure of the men's actual identity. Yet despite this admission, some of the theory's proponents still include his account as a basis for their conclusion that Crockett was executed.

Even the much-cited letter from Sergeant George M. Dolson published in the *Detroit Democratic Free Press* on September 7, 1836—one of the prime documents touted as support for the execution theory—in which

Colonel Juan N. Almonte is supposedly the informant identifying Crockett is fraught with problems. For instance, that Almonte was not the Mexican officer interviewed with Dolson acting as interpreter is clearly provable.

First of all, as a fluent speaker of English, Almonte would have required no interpreter. Secondly, on July 18, 1836, the date of the Dolson interview on Galveston Island, Colonel Almonte was not even present there. He had been removed from San Jacinto and taken to Velasco (present-day Freeport, Texas) more than two months earlier on May 10 and by July 1836 was at the Orozimbo Plantation near West Columbia, Texas, where he was being held prisoner with Santa Anna along with the President's personal secretary, Ramón M. Caro. Moreover, Almonte was later interviewed in the *Philadelphia Pennsylvanian* in 1838 and yet made not a single reference about the Crockett execution, even though rumors regarding it had been swirling throughout the United States and this interview would have been a perfect opportunity to absolve himself from any role in the deed if it had in fact occurred.

The relevant passage in the Dolson letter regarding Crockett reads to this effect: "General Castrillon . . . entered *the back room of the Alamo,* and there found *Crockett and five other* Americans, who had defended it until defence was useless . . . ." (emphasis added). As the six prisoners were marched to Santa Anna's presence, "Colonel Crockett was in the rear, had his arms folded, and appeared bold as the lion as he passed my informant (Almonte.) Santa Anna's interpreter knew Colonel Crockett, and said to my informant, 'the one behind is the famous Crockett.'" Santa Anna then ordered *that the men be shot.*

The critical point is that it is totally unknown who the Mexican officer "informant" was that related the information contained in the Dolson letter—one of the three principal pillars relied upon by the proponents of the Crockett execution story—or whether this person was actually present at the scene of the execution or even at the Alamo battle at all (not all of the Mexican forces at San Jacinto had been in San Antonio at the time of the March 6 conflict). It is entirely possible that whoever furnished this account to Dolson had simply heard the story from someone else and it constituted nothing more than secondhand hearsay—information nonetheless that would serve to ingratiate himself with his Texan captors. Consequently, given these circumstances, the actual probative value of the account in the Dolson letter as evidence for David Crockett's execution is highly questionable at best.

One further point regarding the Dolson account should be addressed. It is believed that on the original handwritten version, George Dolson had inserted the name "Almonte" in parentheses between the lines of the pertinent quoted sentences to correct his oversight in having omitted the name when he had first written the sentences down. It has also been argued that later there was a typesetter's error at the time the letter was printed, and that the name "Almonte" should apply in the quoted sentences to Santa Anna's interpreter (which in fact Almonte was), rather than Almonte being the "informant." When read in that manner, Almonte would be the person who identified Crockett as being one of the prisoners. Admittedly, this could well be the case. However, even if correct, that would still not prove that Crockett was among the executed.

It is undisputed fact that Almonte had been in the United States for extended periods of time, both in 1834 and 1835. It is also a certainty from his own writings that Almonte was well aware of David Crockett's political notoriety in the U.S. during that period—Almonte had even made derogatory comments about Crockett, describing him as a "political lunatic" back in 1834. Granting all of the above, it still does not automatically follow by any means that Almonte would have been able to identify Crockett on sight.

There were of course no photographs available of Crockett in those days. There is also no indication whatsoever that Almonte ever saw Crockett in person during his stays in the United States. It is not impossible that

Almonte could have seen an illustration or even a portrait of David Crockett while in the country, but there is no known evidence nor any suggestion that this ever took place. So it is a real stretch to assume that Almonte would have visually recognized Crockett on March 6, 1836—and such an assumption certainly cannot be considered or utilized as solid proof of Crockett's execution. Furthermore, even if Almonte had thought one of the men to be David Crockett (or actually *did* recognize Crockett), it strains credulity to think that Almonte would have been furtively whispering this fact into the ear of the "informant" instead of immediately conveying this critically important information to Santa Anna himself—regardless of Santa Anna's irate state of mind at that time. (Another Mexican account given the previous month—and confirmed by that of personal secretary Ramón Caro—stated that Santa Anna "flew into a most violent rage" against General Castrillón when presented with the captured prisoners due to the fact that they had not been killed instantly upon their discovery.) Irrespective of Santa Anna's emotional state, Juan Almonte was, after all, the dictator's closest and most trusted personal advisor (and also possibly even Santa Anna's very own nephew).

It is inconceivable that Almonte would have failed to alert Santa Anna that he had in his possession one of the most valuable pawns possible, one that would before the world clinch Santa Anna's case that the United States was violating Mexican sovereignty and inciting a revolution in a brazen land grab of Mexican territory leading to designs of annexation. It was a chance to showcase Crockett as proof of what His Excellency had been saying all along and yet Almonte ineptly allows Santa Anna to let this golden opportunity slip through his fingers by disposing of the best corroborating evidence he could have ever hoped for. That circumstance is simply implausible on its face.

So any way one looks at it, the Dolson account raises more questions than it answers—and it cannot be considered as *definitive* proof of anything.

There is a second account that is regularly relied upon by the proponents of the Crockett execution story. Only a month before Dolson's account, another interview had taken place on June 9, 1836 on Galveston Island—over three full months after Crockett's death—supposedly of a Mexican soldier from the prisoner-of-war camp located there, identified in the account only as the "narrator." This person was apparently interviewed by a correspondent for the *Morning Courier and New-York Enquirer* which included the account in an article published on July 9, 1836. This would be the *very first written account* ever to appear claiming that Crockett was executed. Like Dolson's letter, this narrative also describes the executions following the Alamo battle, including Crockett, but contains several notable differences that contradict statements made in the Dolson account. This article stated that "after the Mexicans had got possession of the Alamo, the fighting had ceased, and it was *clear day light, six* Americans were discovered *near the wall yet unconquered*, and who were instantly surrounded and ordered by Gen. Castrillon to surrender, and who did so . . . . [emphasis added]. He [Castrillón] marched them up to that part of the fort where stood 'His Excellency.'" These particular statements indicate that these prisoners were captured outside of the buildings but within the Alamo compound near one of the defensive walls—and in broad daylight—not discovered hidden away in some back room of the Alamo as stated in the Dolson account. The article then makes the outright claim that "DAVID CROCKETT was one of the six."—with the "narrator" providing nary a hint nor a clue as to how he would have known that as fact.

The article goes on to say that Santa Anna's officers "drew and *plunged their swords* into the bosoms of their defenceless prisoners!!" (emphasis added). It further states that "*three other* wounded prisoners were discovered and brought before 'his Excellency,' and were ordered to be instantly shot."—thus making the total number of executed prisoners *nine rather than six*. (It should be noted here that it is ludicrous to believe that right after Santa Anna's "most violent rage" when the first group of surviving defenders was brought before him that anyone else in his army would have dared to present him with an additional group.)

Neither of the two prior accounts—the Dolson letter nor the *Courier & Enquirer* article—agree on any number of significant details with regard to the execution event, including such facts as how and where the prisoners were captured, whether they were shot or stabbed to death with swords, or even the total number of victims involved. Yet even though they are in serious disparity on the most basic of facts, these are the very accounts that some consider to be gospel proof in regard to their statements that David Crockett was among the men executed.

Like the Dolson letter, this account of Crockett's execution in the *Courier & Enquirer* article is also from a totally unknown, unidentified source—assumedly another unnamed Mexican prisoner. And once again, like the Dolson letter, the probative value of this account concerning Crockett's demise must be considered extremely questionable.

But this could not be categorically or automatically said of the now-famous José Enrique de la Peña diary account, the linchpin and nucleus of all the execution accounts, the key document for scholars of the battle in supporting the claim that Crockett was executed, and it is worth repeating his searing and memorable description of it:

> Very shortly before Santa Anna's speech an unpleasant incident had preceded [it] which, since it happened *after the heat of the melee had already passed* [i.e., the post-battle mayhem and chaos had already ceased and order restored], was considered as a vile murder and contributed greatly to the coolness [following Santa Anna's victory speech] that was noted [emphasis added and translation corrected]. Some seven men had survived the general carnage and, under the protection of General Castrillón, they were brought before Santa Anna. Among them was one of great stature, well proportioned, with regular features, in whose face there was the imprint of adversity, but in whom one also noticed a degree of resignation and nobility that did him honor. He was the naturalist David Croket [*sic*], well known in North America for his unusual adventures, who had undertaken to explore the country and who, finding himself in Béjar at the very moment of surprise, had taken refuge in the Alamo, fearing that his status as a foreigner might not be respected

[this last sentence is suspiciously almost identical to the description of Crockett and the alibi allegedly stated by Crockett upon his capture contained in the account by General Martín Perfecto de Cós that is later discussed.] Santa Anna answered Castrillón's intervention *in Crockett's behalf* [these last three words are not present in Peña's Spanish manuscript] with a gesture of indignation and, addressing himself to the sappers, the troops closest to him, ordered his execution [the original Spanish actually says "ordered that they shoot *them*"— not "ordered *his* execution."] The commanders and officers were outraged at this action and did not support the order, hoping that once the fury of the moment had blown over these men would be spared; but several officers who were around the president and who, perhaps, had not been present during the moment of danger, became noteworthy by an infamous deed, surpassing the soldiers in cruelty. They thrust themselves forward, in order to flatter their commander, and with swords in hand, fell upon these unfortunate, defenseless men just as a tiger leaps upon its prey. They tortured them before killing them, and these unfortunates died moaning, but without humiliating themselves before their executioners. . . . though present, I turned away horrified in order not to witness such a barbarous scene.

In this account the captives, whoever they were (Crockett is the only one named), though executed still die impressively.

But, alas, a close examination of the de la Peña diary brings its own problems and difficulties. As Bill Groneman, Alamo author and investigator, has duly noted, the so-called diary was not a literal diary per se but rather an over 400-page extended memoir created during the years following the war. During his participation in the Texas campaign, Peña had kept a smaller field-note campaign diary and, in Matamoros in the summer of 1836, he transcribed the diary entries to create a compilation consisting of 109 pages. It is very significant to note that in this transcription of the original campaign diary, Peña has no entries whatsoever for the dates of March 3 through March 7 and therefore no mention of the March 6 executions nor of Crockett.

In addition to the diary, to complement his memoir de la Peña had collected not only Mexican newspaper accounts about the Alamo, but also American ones. (Depending on when he came across the newspaper article and decided to add the information could explain why the Crockett execution passage was not included in the original transcription of Peña's diary and did not appear until the later version of his expanded memoir. Although present at the executions, Peña may not have been aware of the claim that one of the victims was David Crockett until he subsequently read it in a newspaper account and therefore decided that he could enhance his memoir by including the famous name in connection with the event. And being a severely harsh critic of Santa Anna, he certainly would have had no compunction about doing so.) The Robert McAlpin Williamson March 1, 1836 letter informing Travis about a sixty-man reinforcement is alluded to by de la Peña in his account, and he may have even gotten hold of, based on some of the language used, a *Davy Crockett's Almanack*. It is known that de la Peña was still working on his memoir at least as late as November 1839.

The salient point here is that the completed memoir did not derive exclusively and instantaneously from the original campaign diary, yet historians have nonetheless treated it all as a spontaneous, on-the-scene account when it was not. To his credit, Peña comes clean in stating that the author (Peña) waited to compile additional material before knitting his narrative together.

Yet, despite this admission by the author himself, Groneman notes that the diary was embraced as if it had directly come out of de la Peña's saddlebag and into the dust jacket of Texas A & M University Press—a 1975 edition where for the first time the Spanish was translated into English by Carmen Perry in which the Crockett execution paragraph caused a firestorm. While the evidence indicates that the Peña account is authentic (something that Groneman strongly challenges because of its provenance and discrepancies), it is not, however, accurate in every detail. This is especially pertinent to the Crockett death narrative.

Lieutenant Colonel José Enrique de la Peña was an officer in Santa Anna's Army of Operations who arrived as one of the Mexican reinforcements at the Alamo on March 3, the tenth day of the siege. He was a talented and brave man with a gift for literary expression—part of the reason his stirring account has been so enthusiastically received by students and scholars of the siege and battle. There is no gainsaying that Peña has contributed mightily to our understanding of what happened that terrible morning of steel and blood, and it deserves our most serious and utmost attention.

But, still, there is a stubborn labyrinth of questions and disconcerting paradoxes that cannot be easily reconciled. The first thing to note is that de la Peña's account of Crockett's death in the collection for his memoir is almost astonishingly brief—confined to a mere two sentences on a single slip of paper. In contrast, in the prior description of Travis's death recorded in Peña's account—and in which he completely misidentified Travis—Peña devoted a full eight sentences. Moreover, the Crockett account itself only appears for the first time as an insertion of that separate single slip of paper into the later expanded version of Peña's manuscript or memoir that consisted of 105 folded quartos of four pages each, strongly indicating that he was adding to his story as he went along. The beginning of the Crockett execution statement was written in a different hand but completed by de la Peña himself. Peña did acknowledge that at some points he was so sick that he had to have assistance by giving parts of his story by dictation to someone else which would account for some of the differences in handwriting that occur in various places in the manuscript.

Furthermore, Peña sometimes augmented his memoir by also inserting new material acquired from other participants in the Texas campaign whom he never identified. Examination of the original de la Peña collection of papers from which his published memoir was derived indicated that the addition and insertion of newly obtained material occurred a number of times. Peña inserted these documents into his own personally written or dictated portions describing the Texas campaign at the appropriate place where they belonged chronologically in the sequence of events.

It was from this combination of de la Peña's own original writings, dictated passages, and the additional inserted material that Jesús Sánchez Garza edited and published the Spanish version of the Peña memoir in Mexico City in 1955. How the Peña collection of papers eventually wound up in Garza's possession over one hundred years later is not known. Unfortunately, de la Peña tragically was killed on October 10, 1840 when a fellow Mexican Army officer who had served in the same unit with him during the Texas campaign, including the attack on the Alamo, fatally stabbed him in the stomach with a sword during a fight based on a political disagreement, and thus Peña never had the opportunity to put the entire manuscript in its final finished form all in his own handwriting nor to ever realize his grand desire of having his work published for the nation to see. He was only thirty-three years old.

Another essential point that must also be remembered about the de la Peña account is that even if personally present at the execution, there is no evidence to indicate nor any reason to believe that Peña himself would have known who David Crockett was or would have recognized him on sight. Even the major proponents of the Crockett execution theory concede that Peña would not have had the ability to recognize Crockett—that he had to have been informed of Crockett's identity by some other person unknown. For that matter, none of the other Mexican military personnel present there on the scene that day would have been able to identify Crockett either, with perhaps only one possible exception, as is discussed elsewhere in this analysis.

De la Peña does not mention the executions, much less David Crockett being among the executed, in his first transcription from the original field-note campaign diary which he completed in the summer of 1836. He also did not mention the executions or Crockett in the pamphlet he published over three years later in 1839. Again, the important thing to note is that Peña does not mention Crockett's death initially, or even early on, but adds this datum only later—much later as it turns out.

That stories of David Crockett's death were the product of rumor mills starting sometime after the battle, and then picked up by others including de la Peña, is believable because the official Mexican reports never mention Crockett being executed, only that like Travis and Bowie, the Alamo's other leaders, he was killed in the battle.

In his first report to Mexico City, written about an hour and a half after the battle, Santa Anna says nothing to Secretary of War José María Tornel about the Crockett execution, only that Crockett's body was "among the corpses," as were those of Travis and Bowie. Nor does he mention anything about Crockett's execution in his more comprehensive account a year later in 1837. Neither does he mention his dramatic encounter with the most famous frontiersman of the 19th century in his autobiography that was published in 1874. This long and uninterrupted stretch of silence is especially curious, since Santa Anna was nothing but zealous in his attempts to bring to light that many of the rebels were American citizens, "perfidious foreigners" as he derisively called them, stirring up insurrection to usurp the rightful Mexican authority over Texas.

In his communication to Secretary of War Tornel, Santa Anna makes a big fuss over a New Orleans Greys flag captured in the Alamo as proof of American treachery. Yet, he is totally reticent about the West's mightiest hunter, a state legislator from Tennessee and someone who served three times as a Congressman in the United States House of Representatives. There is something bizarrely incongruous about championing a captured flag, but not the capture of a live, walking and talking U.S. Congressman fresh out of the United States.

After all, in 1836, there was serious talk of the United States annexing Texas—what better time to unveil the prize of an elective representative who sat in the U.S. Capitol itself and was now caught fighting in an old mission with two hundred other rebels. What a story!—and yet nothing is done to take advantage of it.

Moreover, after the dramatic execution scene that Peña paints with such painful exquisiteness (though he does not claim to witness it—at least in its entirety), as detailed later, Santa Anna asks that the remains of David Crockett be shown to him not once, not twice, but three different times. While one could argue that there is nothing like making sure, this is not only implausible after he himself ordered the execution of Crockett, but it also makes no sense.

Nor does Santa Anna have any reason to cover up the dastardly deed, especially after the far more egregious executions at Goliad just three weeks later where almost four hundred defenseless Texans were mowed down on Palm Sunday in the most depraved and cold-blooded fashion. Santa Anna, as far as he was concerned, had followed the protocols laid out in the Tornel Decree of December 30, 1835 (mandating that all armed "foreigners" who were captured be executed as pirates) and his own dictum, one in which he imperiously enunciated numerous times that "in this war there are no prisoners."

Neither did any of the senior Mexican officers, several of whom left written accounts ever state, although they sought to indict Santa Anna's actions at every turn, anything about Crockett's execution despite the fact that one of them, the literate, educated, and English-speaking Colonel Almonte, kept a day-to-day diary during the siege and the battle. Almonte cites not a single reference about Crockett's execution either then or at any time later during the remaining thirty-three years of his life.

Ramón Martínez Caro, Santa Anna's personal secretary, and therefore one in the know, speaks with disgust of five prisoners being executed by Santa Anna but says nothing about Crockett being among them. Some of these Mexican officers and officials desired Santa Anna's own execution not only for war crimes against the Texans but for his depredations toward his own army—with Caro being one of his bitterest critics. Even so, Caro in his on-the-scene eyewitness account makes absolutely no mention of David Crockett whatsoever. How much more powerful and terrible the indictment against Santa Anna would have been if Caro had reported the colorful frontiersman perishing with those other unfortunates who were brutally executed.

Specifically in regard to his personal account detailing the appalling event (considered by many authorities to be the most reliable and credible of all the Mexican accounts regarding the executions), Caro flatly declared: "We all witnessed this outrage which humanity condemns but which was committed as described. This is a cruel truth, but I cannot omit it." That statement certainly does not seem to indicate that Caro would have hesitated to include Crockett's execution had David Crockett indeed been one of the victims. (And as will be discussed later in this analysis, Caro would have been right at Santa Anna's side when the eyewitness Joe was ordered to identify Crockett's dead body for His Excellency after the battle—*and* the executions—were over. This being the case, Ramón Caro clearly would have been fully aware of whether or not Crockett had been one of the executed defenders.)

General Vicente Filisola, second-in-command of the Mexican army, wrote two accounts, a more abbreviated one in 1838 and then, eleven years later, a more lengthy and comprehensive study about the Texas Revolution and the Alamo. For this memoir he gathered his information from numerous sources, eyewitnesses, and documented material. And, yet he too cites not a single reference about the Crockett execution.

There are even a few Mexican military sources, most notably Captain Rafael Soldaña, a second unnamed Mexican captain, and the Sergeant Félix Núñez account, that clearly describe David Crockett's death in battle, but these accounts were not necessarily any more reliable than those other Mexican sources that alluded to Crockett's execution (though they do however contain some tantalizingly accurate details such as the appearance of Crockett's clothing—buckskin suit and a cap with a long tail, his tall height, as well as giving the same statement that Crockett suffered a disabling gunshot that broke his *right* arm before he was killed fighting, particularly specific and consistent details that would seem unlikely to be pure happenstance).

Colonel Reuben M. Potter, the first historian of the Alamo, would write three separate accounts on the battle, and at the end of the war was at Matamoros where he spoke with Mexican soldiers who had recently fought at the Alamo. Though many of Potter's sources are not specifically identified, no one in the 19th century more thoroughly examined the siege and battle. Potter, who spoke fluent Spanish, agreed that several captives at the Alamo were summarily executed by Santa Anna after the battle, but from his research—which also included interviewing several Mexican participants in the Alamo battle who had remained in Texas after the war—Potter adamantly maintained that Crockett was not among them.

There are even Texan sources, individuals inside the Alamo on the morning of March 6, most notably Susannah Dickinson, Enrique Esparza (eight-year-old son of Alamo defender Gregorio Esparza), and William Travis's slave Joe, who all attest that Crockett died in battle with multiple Mexican casualties around him. But none of them witnessed his death.

The best Mexican source for David Crockett's death remains by far and away the de la Peña account. As stated elsewhere in this analysis, the evidence does not indicate that Peña's writings are a hoax or a forgery. Scientific testing and analysis conducted on the manuscript and published in 2001 by Texas State Archivist David B. Gracy II showed that the paper used was the very same paper utilized by the Mexican Army in 1835–1836 and that the ink was also definitely of that era, thus eliminating the possibility that the Peña document could have been a latter-day forgery.

Moreover, the accuracy of the de la Peña diary wherein he described the specific locations, route, and actions of the Mexican army during the campaign has been fully corroborated by extensive archaeological work conducted by Gregg Dimmick in both Texas and Mexico as is meticulously detailed in his excellent book *Sea of Mud.* In addition, the historian Dr. James E. Crisp's research comparing it with other writing samples of Peña has erased any doubt that the writer of what became *With Santa Anna in Texas* was none other than José Enrique de la Peña.

This is the case despite the work's very shaky provenance after Peña's death and some unknown sources he used, as well as the strikingly similar language Peña employs in describing Crockett's execution to that contained in a 1904 letter by historian William Zuber regarding the same event. In this letter Zuber relates information that Dr. George M. Patrick had extracted from General Martín Perfecto de Cós (who led part of the attack on the Alamo) while Cós was a captive of the Texans at San Jacinto, and which Zuber admits was a gross falsehood on Cós's part.

DAVID CROCKETT'S DEATH 53

In his account, Cós claimed that when he discovered Crockett, the Tennessean had stated to him, "I have come to Texas on a visit of exploration.... And here I am yet, a noncombatant and foreigner, having taken no part in the fighting." The parallel of expression in the Cós and the earlier-quoted Peña account appears too close to be a mere coincidence. In actuality, David Crockett was an experienced woodsman and hunter—not a "naturalist" or scientific "explorer" roaming around the country like John James Audubon collecting biological specimens.

(A possible explanation for the similarity between the de la Peña and the Cós account described by Zuber may be that during the years following the war, Peña also heard the same story from either Cós himself or someone else who had heard Cós's story and Peña incorporated elements of it into his narrative.)

Zuber made the point about Cós's account not being true because he wanted to show how easily the lies of idle talkers may find their way into history. Ironically, Zuber was also thought to be an idle talker and Walter Lord, author of the acclaimed Alamo book *A Time to Stand*, called him an incorrigible raconteur, but this was only partially correct—William Zuber's *My Eighty Years in Texas* is a noteworthy body of work profitably used by historians and scholars today.

One prime example of why the account by Cós is considered totally unreliable: In his account, Cós claims that he himself was the one who personally found David Crockett (and Crockett *alone*) locked up in one of the rooms of the Alamo barracks and tried to save his life. All other accounts state that the Mexican officer who discovered the hidden defenders and attempted to intervene on their behalf was General Manuel F. Castrillón. It is highly likely that Cós concocted this tale about Crockett in order to endear himself to the Texans, most of whom bitterly hated Cós because of his violation of the parole granted him following his surrender of Béxar in December of 1835. As a result, the Texans were strongly urging Cós's execution along with that of Santa Anna.

As quoted previously, the Cós account contains several ridiculous and outlandish statements allegedly made to him by Crockett upon his discovery, e.g., Crockett said he had been merely exploring the country and was caught totally unawares in the Alamo at the time the Mexican Army arrived in San Antonio, he had taken no part in the fighting, and so forth. In addition, the account by Cós even asserts that upon the order of his execution, Crockett had lunged at Santa Anna with a dagger in an attempt to kill him. The fact that de la Peña would include spurious statements from a source of such dubious nature in his Crockett execution narrative certainly fails to engender confidence in the accuracy of the Peña account regarding Crockett's death.

One additional circumstance may be relevant to the *Courier,* Dolson, and Cós accounts. In an article by author Bill Groneman entitled "Follow the Money" published in the *Alamo Journal* (Issue No. 172, August 2014), Groneman brought out the fact that the reporter who wrote the *Courier & Enquirer* article (and his New York editor), the author of the Dolson letter (and the Texan officer who ordered Dolson to translate the Mexican officer interview), and Dr. George M. Patrick, the man who related the Cós account, were all members or close associates involved in a Texas land scheme named the New Washington Association (NWA). This organization had raised the money and built the town of New Washington just south of San Jacinto which Santa Anna and Almonte had burnt to the ground on April 20, 1836—the day prior to the decisive battle.

Following the Mexican defeat at San Jacinto, the members of the NWA greatly desired the death of Santa Anna, not only as revenge for his destruction of their valuable property and goods, but more importantly to forever prevent his return to Mexico where he could initiate a second invasion of Texas which would avert or at least delay their goal to have Texas ceded to the United States and thereby protect their investment. As a result of San Jacinto, Santa Anna, Almonte, and Cós became prisoners of the Texans.

Shortly following the battle—and during the same timeframe and location in which the three above-referenced accounts of Crockett's execution originated—the NWA members and their associates embarked on a campaign in which they vociferously and publicly advocated for the trial and execution of Santa Anna. Correspondence among them during this period shows that they were intricately connected and in frequent communication in furtherance of that end.

The circumstances described above could well be more than mere coincidence regarding the root of these three particular Crockett execution accounts so damning to Santa Anna—the first two of which being not only the very first written accounts of Crockett's execution to ever appear (both sources totally anonymous), but also two of the three principal pillars that the Crockett execution proponents rely on to support the execution theory. (All of the specific names involved, their interrelationships, and the full documentation thereof are contained in Groneman's article cited above.)

Much of the subsequent focus on the manner of Crockett's death on March 6 likely arose in large part due to the fact that he met his fate right in the midst of an extremely tumultuous period. Part of the hysteria existing at the time was that events were transpiring so rapidly (the Alamo, Goliad, and San Jacinto, terrifying and shattering events, all occurred within a matter of six weeks) that Texas became flooded with all sorts of rumors, gossip, and innuendo, many of which concerned David Crockett. His fame made him omnipresent—an Everyman for every situation.

Let us count the ways all these different scenarios and rumors (several not even concerning his death) have wildly circulated around the person of David Crockett:

- He was one of the prisoners who were executed after the battle.
- He died after killing scores of Mexican soldiers who lay around his prostrate body.
- He was the last to die at the Alamo.
- He was the first to die on the morning of March 6.
- He personally negotiated terms with Santa Anna during the siege.
- He drew the line in the sand.
- He left the Alamo and brought back a second reinforcement contingent.
- He was killed by a Mexican lancer along with others who died on the plains.
- And, yes, he survived the battle and was a prisoner in the salt mines of Mexico.

All these scenarios had one thing in common, Davy Crockett—he was larger than life—everything seemed to happen around him simply because he was Crockett.

So, the rumor mill churned and churned around this charismatic figure and nearly two hundred years after the battle it has not abated.

Crockett himself acknowledged this phenomenon when he wrote in the preface to his 1834 memoir (and in his own inimitable style) that

> I know . . . my name is making a considerable deal of fuss in the world. I can't tell . . . in what it is to end. Go where I will, everybody seems anxious to get a peep at me; and it would be hard to tell which would have the advantage, if I, and the "Government," and "Black Hawk" [prominent West Tennessee lawyer and politician Adam Huntsman], and a great eternal big caravan of wild varments were all to be showed at the same time in four different parts of any of the big cities in the nation. I am not so sure that I shouldn't get the most custom [patronage] of any of the crew [group]. There must therefore be something in me, or about me, that attracts attention . . . .

But let us turn back to de la Peña and his diary on another curiosity. In his account he also vividly portrays another remarkable death scene—one just as compelling as David Crockett's demise—but this one involves William Barret Travis, the other critical figure in the battle, the very soul and embodiment of defiance at the Alamo. Of course, Travis's death could not be neglected and must be described with the same burning and searing language. Like Crockett's demise, Peña's gripping description of the only other famous defender fighting in the battle is worth repeating verbatim. Peña's sprawling narrative dramatically picks up at the moment the Mexican army overruns the walls, and the defenders are forced to retreat to the Long Barracks as a second line of defense:

> . . . Not all of them took refuge, for some remained in the open, looking at us before firing, as if dumbfounded at our daring. Travis was seen to hesitate, but not about the death that he would choose. He would take a few steps and stop, turning his proud face toward us to discharge his shots; he fought like a true soldier. Finally he died, but he died after having traded his life very dearly. None of his men died with greater heroism, and they all died. . . . He was a handsome blond, with a physique as robust as his spirit was strong.

By any measure a remarkable death scene. There is no doubt that some defender of the Alamo died in this heroic fashion—it just was not William Barret Travis.

Travis's slave Joe, who survived the battle and is described by those who knew him as intelligent and credible, stood right next to Travis on the North Wall, and stated quite clearly that after discharging his shotgun at the approaching enemy, a shot rang out in the semidarkness felling Travis, at which point he became one of the first Texan casualties of the battle.

Captain José Juan Sánchez-Navarro, a leader in the Mexican attack on the Alamo's northern front, also stated that Colonel Travis had died on the North Wall and identified his body after the battle, as did then-Mayor of San Antonio de Béxar, Francisco Antonio Ruíz. So, Peña is dead wrong in describing the only other celebrity death, so to speak, in the Alamo—and the only other defender from the battle that he names. Even Peña's physical description of Travis as a "handsome blond" with a "robust physique" is at variance with Travis's known appearance.

These mistakes regarding William Travis must detract from the veracity of de la Peña's description of David Crockett's vivid and graphic death. If he had been testifying in a court of law, the fact that he got the death of one famous defender so wrong would cast powerful doubts among any fair-minded jury that he got the other one right—especially considering the flourishing prose attached to both.

Imparting a famous name to these two victims immeasurably adds to the drama and intensity of the story. Peña appeared to be a writer that hungered for detail, but one that was also gripped with a poetic imagination—which is why some portions of his narrative may be generally right but not specifically accurate in every particular or attribute.

It is why, in his article "The Death of David Crockett," the author Michael Lind, in analyzing the death accounts of Crockett, stated that both the de la Peña and Dolson accounts followed the 19th-century rules of popular fiction in which part of the drama includes the two most famous antagonists having a chance meeting. Just like Travis's death it was not enough that someone of David Crockett's stature, who was vested with such celebrity and importance during his lifetime, die anonymously (heroes, for God's sake, cannot die anonymously); it must be someone with equal importance, at least in terms of infamy—a villain of historic proportions—that had to execute the Alamo's most famous defender. Who better, argues Lind, than Santa Anna?

And as author James Donovan astutely observed, "... before the invention of electronic recording devices around the turn of the 20th century, history was more pliable, especially for those with an agenda—or simply to make a good story even better."

There is one basic, common-sense reason why the Crockett execution story is highly doubtful—the situational reality of the battle that was raging. If Crockett was in fact involved in the fighting, regardless of the location, in the extremely chaotic and hand-to-hand mayhem taking place there, simple logic indicates that he would have had almost no imaginable opportunity to surrender and be taken prisoner—virtually impossible.

The only conceivable way that Crockett could have been taken *alive* is if he had been in some back room hidden away completely concealed from view along with the group of defenders who actually were captured well after the fighting was over (as will be discussed later). This would be totally out of character from everything we know about David Crockett, and certainly does not comport with the various descriptions of his prior behavior during battle. The only way one can surmise about Crockett's actions on the morning of March 6 is by his past actions. The past, as has been said, is prologue and it is documented what Crockett did at the only other time the Mexican army attacked the Alamo in force—he acted as the leading spirit in its defense.

Following the Mexican Army's attempt to storm the south wall of the Alamo on the morning of February 25—during which the Texans endured a two-hour constant hail of artillery and musket fire—in his after-action report to Major General Samuel Houston (Commander-in-Chief of the Army of Texas), Colonel William Travis specifically singled out Crockett's leadership in the day's conflict stating the following: "The Hon[orable] David Crockett was seen at all points, animating the men to do their duty." Certainly not the actions of a man who would have sought refuge on March 6, 1836, cowering back in some dark room of the mission in an effort to hide from the enemy as some critics would have it. Nor would such conduct align with the numerous earlier accounts of Crockett's valor fighting in the 1814 Creek War while serving under the command of General Andrew Jackson.

Here is what Alamo survivor (and eyewitness to Crockett's mangled corpse lying in front of the Church) Enrique Esparza had to say about what David Crockett had done both during the twelve-day siege and the final fateful battle: "I remember Crockett." "Crockett seemed to be the leading spirit." "He was always at the head." ". . . He was everywhere during the siege . . . ." "He went to every exposed point and personally directed the fighting." "He fought hand to hand." And finally, ". . . He fought to his last breath." Having been sequestered in the Sacristy in the back of the Alamo Church during the final battle, these last two statements by Esparza obviously constituted a logically inferred conclusion drawn from the conditions and circumstances in which he had seen Crockett's dead body when he was being led out of the Church as the violence of the battle was subsiding on the morning of March 6.

In attempting to determine the truth in this whole question regarding the death of David Crockett it may well be useful and appropriate to apply the established principle and rule of analysis known as "Ockham's razor," i.e., that the simplest of two or more competing theories is preferable and more likely to be correct.

It only takes one person to start a rumor. It is quite possible—even likely—that the initial genesis of the Crockett execution story was as simple as this: One Mexican (perhaps Dolson's "informant," whoever that was) mistakenly thought that some other buckskin-clad defender he saw executed was David Crockett and said so. All of the subsequent tales of Crockett's execution flowed from that.

Numerous unsubstantiated accounts (many obviously bogus on their face) cannot be simply stacked up in a pile and then characterized as constituting an overwhelming body of evidence for Crockett's execution as some of the theory's proponents have attempted to do ever since the very beginning of this controversy. Simply put, whether you have two pieces of flawed, unreliable evidence or twenty pieces of flawed, unreliable evidence—it is still all flawed, unreliable evidence.

It is the quality of the evidence that is of significance, not the quantity.

In summary, there are simply too many questions, contradictions, uncertainties, and unknowns regarding the accounts purporting Crockett's execution to draw from them any firm or reliable conclusion as to the manner of Crockett's death.

Having reviewed and evaluated the sources and evidence that have been used to support the Crockett execution theory, two essential elements regarding the subject of David Crockett's death remain to be presented and analyzed—neither of which has ever been previously considered throughout the course of the entire debate, and either one of which, if proven to be factual, renders Crockett's execution an absolute impossibility.

A Comprehensive Analysis of the Controversy:
Presenting the New Evidence

A preliminary explanation of the techniques employed in this analysis. In attempting to solve the question of the manner of David Crockett's death, it became obvious that a new approach was necessary if a truly reliable conclusion could ever be reached. As has been demonstrated in the first half of the book, ever since it arose the debate on this issue has for the most part been a never-ending battle of dueling witness accounts supporting one side or the other—a battle that could go on forever with no definitive resolution.

For this analysis, we have adopted a different approach—one that uses established techniques commonly employed in the solving of cold case murders and other crimes. These techniques include a thorough examination of all the extant testimony and a determination of the relative weight that should be assigned to that testimony based on the credibility of the particular witness who gave it determined by a number of factors.

These include:
- Is the identity of that witness known to a certainty.
- Was the witness in fact present at the scene of the event.
- Would the witness have been in a position or physical location such that he could have seen what he claimed to see.
- Were the light conditions or any physical obstructions such that he could have seen what he claimed to see.
- Is it reasonable to believe that the witness could or would have known the identity of the person that he claimed to identify.

These and other factors were all taken into account in attempting to determine the weight each witness and his testimony should be given.

Some of the questions this analysis attempted to answer were these.

<u>Who</u>:
1. Who was the person identified as Crockett in the particular accounts—actually Crockett or someone else.
2. Who was the person who made the identification. Would this person have known who Crockett was and would this person have had the ability to recognize Crockett on sight.

What:
1. What were the existing circumstances (order versus chaos, light conditions, and so forth) at the time and place of Crockett's death.
2. What were the physical conditions (physical circumstances) surrounding Crockett's dead body.
3. What were the physical conditions (physical circumstances) at the site where the execution of the captured Alamo defenders occurred.

When:
1. When in the timeline occurrence of events on March 6, 1836 did Crockett die.
2. When did the execution of the captured Alamo defenders occur.
3. When did the noncombatant survivors who were sequestered inside of the Church leave the Alamo.
4. When did Santa Anna enter the Alamo.
5. When on March 6, 1836 did the various witnesses see Crockett's dead body.
6. When and under what circumstances did the various witnesses make their statements claiming to have seen Crockett's dead body.

Where:
1. Where in the Alamo compound did Crockett die.
2. Where in the Alamo compound did the execution of the captured Alamo defenders occur.
3. Where in the Alamo compound was Crockett's dead body located as indicated by the various witnesses.

Why:
What were the possible or probable motives of each person who gave an account of Crockett's death or who provided an account purportedly given by someone else.

How:
1. How would any of the Mexican troops at the Alamo have been able to identify Crockett on sight or even know who he was.
2. How could these directly contradictory and opposing accounts of Crockett's death have come about.

During the course of this investigation the attempt was made to get accurate and reliable answers to each of the preceding questions and others based upon all of the available evidence. The evidence employed in this analysis consists not only of the testimony of valid eyewitnesses, but also the consideration of valid and pertinent circumstantial evidence.

In regard to the latter, circumstantial evidence is sometimes dismissed as unsubstantial or even meaningless. This belief is evidently held by a good many people. One will hear statements such as, "That doesn't count for anything—it's just circumstantial," and similar remarks of that nature.

Although this may be an opinion widely held, it is directly contrary to the facts. Untold numbers of people have been convicted of serious crimes, including murder, entirely on the basis of circumstantial evidence alone. Circumstantial evidence can be quite powerful, sometimes even more strongly convincing and probative than direct eyewitness testimony. For example, if you wake up and see snow on the ground in the morning and there was none there when you went to sleep the night before, that is virtually irrefutable evidence—albeit circumstantial—that it snowed during the night, even though you did not actually see it snowing. The strength of circumstantial evidence depends upon the relevance of the circumstance to the particular subject in question, and upon the strength of the evidence supporting the fact that the circumstance existed. Consequently, valid circumstantial evidence has been considered as a factor where it is relevant and material to the question at issue in this analysis.

As an example in validation of the above, the following statements from the Judicial Council of California Criminal Jury Instructions confirm that legally there is *no* qualitative distinction between direct (eyewitness) and circumstantial (indirect) evidence in a case: "Both direct and circumstantial evidence are acceptable types of evidence to prove or disprove the elements of a charge . . . and neither is necessarily more reliable than the other. Neither is entitled to any greater weight than the other."

Concerning the burden or standards of proof. In a civil case the burden of proof standard is "Proven by a preponderance of the evidence," i.e., the weight of the evidence tilts slightly in favor of one side or the other. Or simply put—a certain conclusion is more likely than not.

In a criminal case the standard of proof is "Proven beyond a reasonable doubt"—a higher bar. This standard in a legal setting has been defined as "Based solely upon the testimony and evidence presented at trial, this conclusion is the one at which a reasonable person would arrive," with "reasonable person" being defined as a person having common sense. Or in other words—after seeing and hearing all of the evidence presented, a person with common sense would reach this conclusion.

Note that the standard requires that the conclusion reached be beyond a reasonable, common-sense doubt— not beyond any *possible* doubt, a level of certainty that is virtually never attainable, no matter how strong the evidence.

In consideration of the above definitions, we believe the testimony and evidence presented in this analysis supporting our conclusion has met both of these standards.

To begin this investigation: One of the critical—potentially even conclusive—pieces of overlooked evidence continues to be totally unrecognized in this whole drama in determining the circumstances of David Crockett's death, although the lead author first raised it all the way back in 1987. And that pertains to Susannah Dickinson, a pivotal eyewitness and a major primary source, who saw Crockett dead and mutilated—and as the evidence will show—*before Santa Anna ever entered the fort.*

The specific timeline of the occurrence of events that took place on the morning of March 6, 1836 is one key factor that should prove to be dispositive in the whole complex and tangled Crockett execution controversy. Given the multiplicity of existing conflicting accounts, contradictory evidence, diverse interpretations, and contentious arguments, the accurate determination of the particular sequence of events is one of the *only* possible means by which a final, reliable conclusion can ever be reached.

This essential piece of the puzzle has never been addressed (or even alluded to) at any point during which the controversy has raged since the de la Peña diary first appeared in 1975. This is surprisingly the case despite the voluminous amount of disputation and debate found in the plethora of books, articles, and papers that this subject has generated. By all indications, the crucial timeline element as it relates to the issue of Crockett's death has never undergone a comprehensive, thoroughgoing examination and analysis until now.

Mrs. Susannah Dickinson states, quite unambiguously, in the 1874 James M. Morphis account, which Todd Hansen (widely acknowledged expert authority on the analysis of Alamo witness accounts) rates as strong and highly credible—an unfiltered direct quotation straight from Dickinson herself—that while she was being hurriedly escorted out of the Alamo, "As we passed through the enclosed ground in front of the church, I saw heaps of dead and dying. . . . I recognized Col. Crockett lying dead and mutilated between the church and the two story barrack building [the Long Barracks], and even remember seeing his peculiar cap lying by his side."

It is a descriptive line that appears straightforward, honest, and without the usual editorial embellishment often found in other Alamo accounts. This is critically important (and as author Walter Lord said she seemed incapable of flights of fancy) because the evidence indicates that Mrs. Dickinson saw Crockett's corpse before Santa Anna ever entered the fort. If this is true, and the facts strongly argue in its favor, it would then be impossible for Santa Anna to order the execution of someone who was already dead regardless of the circumstances surrounding his death.

There is an additional Dickinson account not given until very late in her life when she was aged and ill and not published until 1901, eighteen years after her death, that gives a slightly different location for Crockett's body. (Hansen rated this particular account as being by far the weakest of all the accounts Dickinson ever gave about her experience in the Alamo.) In this her final version she stated that "she found Crockett lying dead in a little confessional room in the Northeast corner of the Alamo [church], with a huge pile of dead Mexicans lying around him." The Confessional was the first room to the left after entering the Church—north of the front door of the Church and east of its front wall.

This location would be consistent with a number of Mexican soldier accounts (those of Captain Rafael Soldaña and another unnamed Mexican captain in particular) that describe David Crockett as fighting inside the doorway of a small room bashing Mexican troops with his rifle until it broke off at the stock, he was shot in the right arm, and Crockett then continued swinging the barrel of the rifle using his left arm until finally being killed. (In some of these Mexican accounts a large, long knife in addition to the rifle was also used by Crockett in his final fight.)

Going from Mrs. Dickinson's refuge in the Sacristy room to the front part of the Church, due to the location of the long cannon ramp that ran from just inside the front door of the Church all the way back to the Church's rear artillery platform, Dickinson would have had to pass right by the doorway of the Confessional. (See Figure 1.)

The evidence suggests that Crockett's actions on the morning of March 6 could have been as follows:

Colonel Crockett and his men had originally been assigned to defend the South Palisade. However, on March 6 the Mexicans attempted no attack at the South Palisade. Instead, they launched a direct assault on the Alamo's Lunette and Main Gate, at which time Crockett's force shifted to defend the Main Gate behind the thick barrier of sandbags located there. When the Mexicans surmounted the Alamo's southwest corner, defense of the Main Gate became untenable. Crockett fell back to a defensive position in front of the Church, and was either killed there, or was possibly forced to reposition inside the Church and he went to the first room on the left—the Confessional. (Based on the totality of the evidence this last possibility is much less likely than that Crockett was killed outside.)

Whichever location is actually correct, the key point is that Susannah Dickinson did, at least twice,

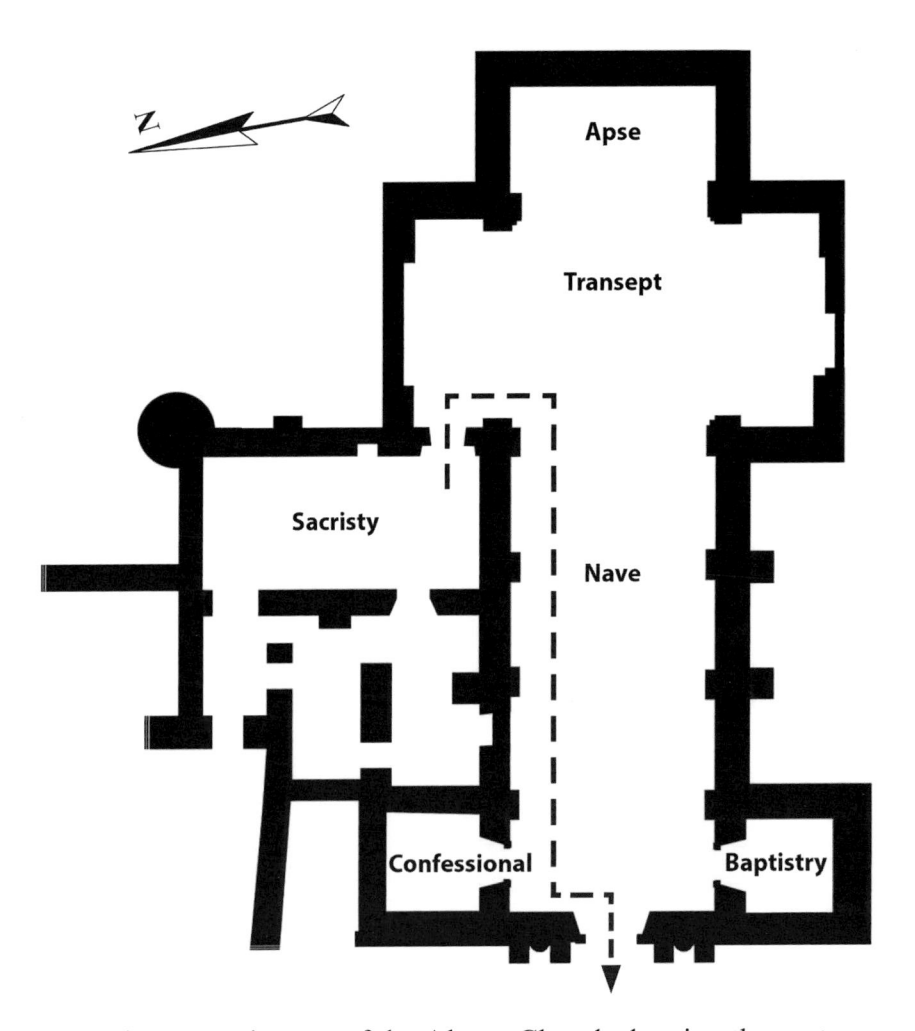

Figure 1. Diagram of the Alamo Church showing the route Susannah Dickinson took in going from the Sacristy, alongside the north wall of the Nave, past the doorway of the Confessional, and exiting through the front doorway.

whether inside or outside of the Church, report seeing Crockett's dead body as she was being led out of the Alamo. Enrique Esparza left the Church at the same time as Mrs. Dickinson, and he also placed Crockett's body right outside the Church. (The description given in the third referenced Mexican account, that of Sergeant Félix Núñez, appears to be consistent with the Texan accounts indicating that Crockett had been killed fighting outside in the area in front of the Church.) (See Figure 2.)

That Dickinson could have been mistaken about his identity is highly improbable since David Crockett was a celebrity and, just like today, would have invited more scrutiny from others. He was never one known for his anonymity. Mrs. Dickinson not only saw and knew Crockett ever since his arrival in Béxar on February 8, nearly a month before the climactic battle—but the famous frontiersman took lodging at the Músquiz house in downtown San Antonio de Béxar, the very same house in which Dickinson also resided up to the day of the siege, and she had even laundered Crockett's clothing and that of his Tennessee companions. Moreover, by her own testimony, Dickinson spoke to him face to face multiple times both before and during the siege. Crockett had even, she tells us, sought her out on several occasions.

On the morning of the battle, Susannah Dickinson had no trouble identifying Alamo defenders Galba Fuqua,

Robert Evans, and Jacob Walker—all of whom she saw killed or seriously wounded while in the midst of an extremely traumatic situation—and historians for the most part have unquestionably accepted her identifications of those individuals. Being able to recognize people you know has nothing to do with literacy or level of education. Given her degree of familiarity with Crockett, it is therefore highly probable that the man she identified as the dead Crockett, even citing his peculiar cap by his side, was indeed David Crockett and not someone else.

Using that as a basis, let us review the circumstances surrounding her departure from the Alamo that morning which only strengthen the conclusion that she had already left the fort prior to Santa Anna's arrival. The reason Mrs. Dickinson was quickly escorted out of the fort was because the Mexican army at that time was literally in a mad frenzy, repeatedly shooting and mutilating the defenders' dead bodies. After a long, gruelling, and exhausting journey of hundreds of miles to San Antonio de Béxar under the harshest conditions; and after thirteen days of pent-up siege; a furious morning battle fought mostly in semidarkness, a struggle in which they saw hundreds of their comrades slaughtered and maimed outside the dreaded walls and inside the compound, the Mexican army was in a bloodlust after they now had their hated enemy at their mercy. It was a scene of utter chaos and mayhem.

81

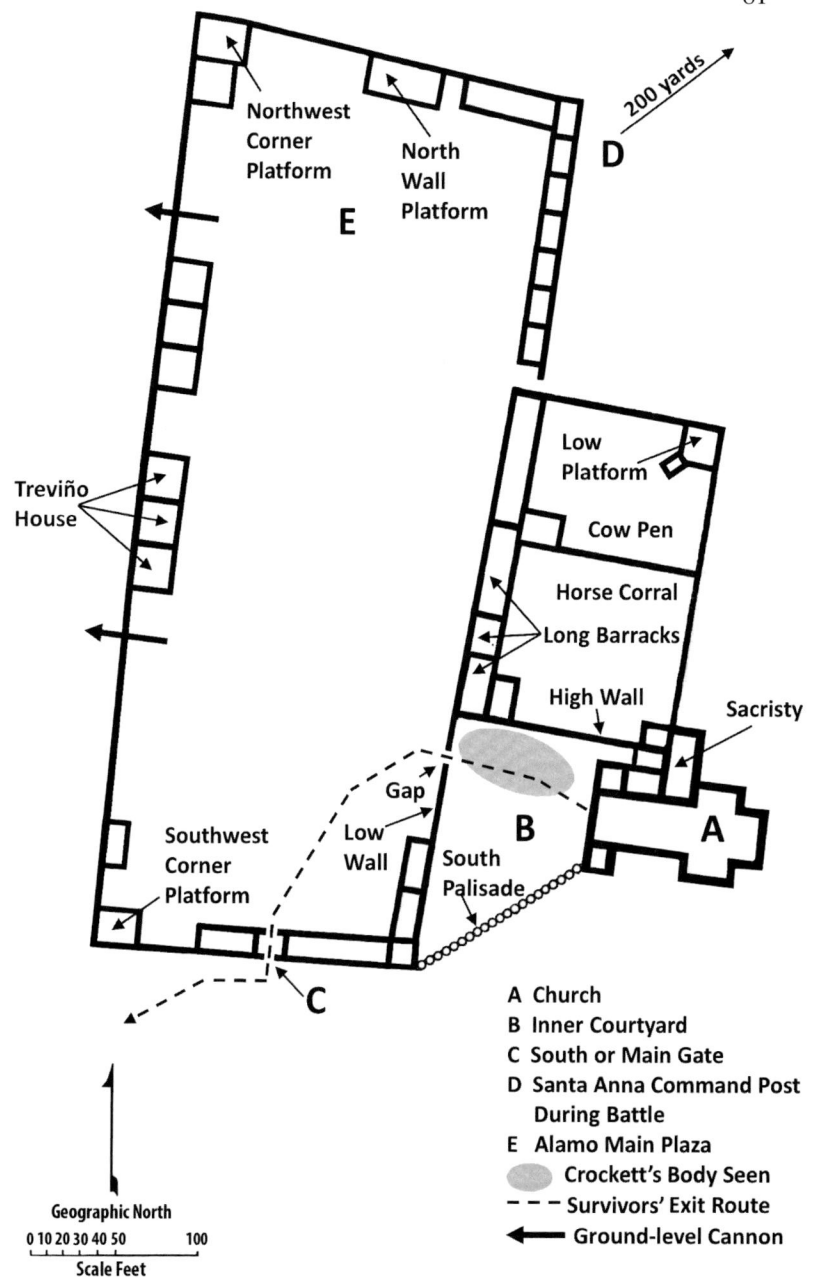

Figure 2. The entire Alamo compound showing the area in which the bona fide eyewitnesses identified Crockett's body.

Dickinson was being rushed out to ensure her safety and that of the other women and children since the army was in the throes of uncontrollable savagery. We also know that Santa Anna had made a promise to Señora María Francisca Músquiz (wife of Ramón Músquiz, Santa Anna acquaintance and former political chief of the Department of Texas) who lived in Béxar and knew Susannah Dickinson who had been living with her in the Músquiz house. Señora Músquiz had pleaded with Santa Anna to save Mrs. Dickinson's life. The General told her that he would do what he could to spare the Alamo women and children.

That is why an English-speaking Mexican officer, twice identified in Dickinson's later accounts as Colonel Juan Almonte, raced into the Church and called for Mrs. Dickinson specifically by name—he knew her name because of Señora Músquiz's plea to Santa Anna—telling Dickinson quite pointedly it was a matter of life and death. And indeed, it was. The now half-crazed soldados had, before Mrs. Dickinson's very presence in the dark side room of the Sacristy in the Church, bayonetted an unarmed twelve-year-old boy who had merely thrown a blanket over his shoulder.

And this was not the only horrendous act of violence that she had witnessed firsthand. Suddenly, three of the gunners from the Church battery, frantically seeking to escape the attacking Mexicans, had run into the Sacristy and were shot down, their bodies landing almost at her feet. Artilleryman Jacob Walker was among the last to fall. Already wounded and streaming blood, Walker staggered into the Sacristy and took refuge in a dark corner opposite Susannah. Mexican soldiers burst into the room and within seconds he was discovered. As reported in the *San Antonio Express* in 1881, Mrs. Dickinson recalled seeing Walker bayonetted and viciously tortured by four Mexicans who repeatedly lifted him up in the air "like a farmer does a bundle of fodder with his pitchfork. . . ." The pitiful victim was then shot dead. The superstitious Mexicans had even killed a cat for no other reason than they believed that it was really "an American."

As Susannah Dickinson was bustled outside from the relative darkness of the Church and into the compound that was now being illuminated by the early dawn light, the Mexican troops, according not only to Dickinson and Enrique Esparza but also the testimony of several Mexican officers, continued to slaughter wounded defenders and to shoot at and bayonet dead bodies. The violent frenzy was yet in full fury. With a small child wrapped in her arms, even though under the close protection of Colonel Almonte, Mrs. Dickinson was still wounded, shot through the right leg between the knee and ankle.

Along with Dickinson, at least fourteen (and possibly as many as seventeen) other people were escorted from inside the Church and out of the Alamo with her, but not one of them reported seeing any sign of Santa Anna that morning, nor he them. This is important in constructing a timeline of the events especially in terms of Santa Anna's arrival inside the fort. Would not such a parade of survivors have attracted the attention of El Presidente if he was indeed present—or would not one of them have seen him?

Santa Anna's interest in the survivors was consuming, having promptly summoned them before him that very same afternoon—questioning the Mexican captives about why they were fighting against their own people. He even offered, to Mrs. Dickinson's abject horror, to adopt her little girl, Angelina, the so-called babe of the Alamo, to raise her in Mexico. Colonel Almonte somehow managed to talk him out of it.

Santa Anna also had a purpose in keeping some noncombatants alive—he wanted to make sure that these eyewitnesses spread the word of the terrible fate of those who had the foolhardy temerity to oppose him. So, yes, Santa Anna was definitely interested in these survivors, but in the early morning of March 6 he was still somewhere outside beyond the North Wall where he had been positioned at the outset and throughout the course of the battle. That area was at the opposite end of the Alamo compound from where the noncombatants were escorted outside through the South (or Main) Gate to various locations in the town as shown in Figure 2.

There is another point worth noting. Travis's slave Joe was secreted in the Treviño house, Travis's officer quarters located almost directly opposite across the Alamo Main Plaza from where Mrs. Dickinson was led out of the Church. In spite of this fact, by all accounts Joe and Dickinson did not see each other that morning of March 6. They certainly knew one another. In fact, Joe was present in the same room at the time Santa Anna interviewed Susannah Dickinson about three o'clock that afternoon. And then two days later on March 8, while out on the prairie on her journey to Gonzales, Dickinson encountered Joe (having escaped the night of the 6th) who was hiding in the tall grass fearful of Mexicans pursuing him, and he happily joined her, the babe, and Almonte's cook, Benjamin "Ben" Harris, whom El Presidente had chivalrously arranged for an escort.

On the morning of March 6, the reason Mrs. Dickinson had not espied Joe after the battle was that he was not discovered until after she had already been escorted from the fort. Even though at the time Joe attempted to surrender, a Mexican soldier purposely shot at him and nicked him in the side with a piece of buckshot, it was now later in the morning and the pandemonium had mostly dissipated.

Santa Anna's interest in survivors was obviously intense. That is why Joe, a survivor, was brought immediately to General Santa Anna once he arrived inside the fort as were the executed prisoners immediately upon their discovery. Santa Anna was interested in survivors even if he wanted them killed. The fact that the fifteen to eighteen survivors escorted from the Church were not brought directly to Santa Anna is one more indication that at the time they were led out of the Alamo he had not yet made his grand and victorious entry into the fort.

When Joe was brought before Santa Anna, he reports no sign of the widespread chaos, no shooting and bayonetting of dead bodies that Mrs. Dickinson and Esparza had so vividly noted. The whole atmosphere and disposition of the troops had remarkably and dramatically changed. By the time that Santa Anna came into the Alamo, the troops had fallen back into their ranks. It makes total sense that Santa Anna would enter the Alamo later rather than earlier since it was a big place, and a sniper could be hiding anywhere to take a pot shot at the Napoleon of the West. (Indeed, an account from historian Reuben Potter actually states that when Santa Anna had initially attempted to enter the fort, "he was greeted by a few shots from the upper part of the chapel [the Alamo Church]" and His Excellency quickly reversed course.)

De la Peña's narrative supports this change in circumstance:

> This scene of extermination had gone on for close to an hour when the curtain of death covered and ended it: shortly after six in the morning it was all finished; *the corps began to form up and had begun to identify themselves, . . . when the general in chief presented himself.* [emphasis added].

This statement clearly underscores that order had been restored by the time Santa Anna entered the Alamo—a far cry from the bloodthirsty mania that was taking place when Susannah Dickinson was earlier escorted out of the Church and when she then saw the dead Crockett.

The description by de la Peña quoted above also ties in with Santa Anna personal secretary Ramón Caro's testimony that when General Manuel F. Castrillón (who would later be killed at the Battle of San Jacinto, thus leaving history no account) brought the prisoners before Santa Anna, he was severely reprimanded for not having killed them immediately upon their discovery, after which Santa Anna turned his back upon Castrillón "while the soldiers *stepped out of their ranks* [notice they were in formation, arrayed in ranks] and set upon the prisoners until they were all killed." (emphasis added).

To arrange a military body into ranks translates into an expression of orderliness, organization, discipline, and uniformity—the very antithesis of what Dickinson and Enrique Esparza had earlier witnessed. This is the proper disposition for troops when the Commander-in-Chief appears before them. Note in particular that this description by Ramón Caro and the one quoted above from de la Peña indicate that *the executions took place in the same location in which the troops were formed up in ranks.* The critical significance of this fact will be demonstrated later in this analysis.

As further confirmation that the executions occurred after Susannah Dickinson and the other noncombatant survivors had already left the Alamo is a key piece of evidence furnished by Reuben Potter. One of Potter's sources was a Mexican sergeant who worked for Potter after the war as a servant in Texas for several years, and this soldier had personally witnessed the Alamo executions, as had a number of Potter's other sources. Potter wrote that the executed men were found concealed in one of the rooms under some mattresses and that they were discovered *"half an hour or more after the action was over."*(emphasis added). The presence of the mattresses explains why the hidden defenders had not been found immediately when the Mexican soldiers were storming through the rooms killing but instead were only discovered significantly later well after order had been restored.

This sequence of events as related by Reuben Potter is strongly corroborated by that given in Ramon Caro's account wherein he stated that "among the 183 killed there were five who were discovered by General Castrillón *hiding after the assault.* He took them immediately to the presence of His Excellency *who had come up by this time.*" (emphasis added).

The circumstances surrounding the discovery of these defenders is in no way indicative that they were cowardly. General Castrillón himself called them "brave men," and Lieutenant Colonel de la Peña specifically pointed out that these prisoners refused to humiliate themselves before their executioners. Furthermore, these men had resolutely persevered in the face of overwhelming odds, withstanding attack and siege for thirteen days, and if given the opportunity, it is always more effectual to the cause to attempt to survive and live to fight another day once there no longer exists any viable means to resist—in fact it is mandated in the present-day United States Armed Forces Code of Conduct.

Meanwhile, the argument that Mrs. Dickinson was delusional, only imagined she saw David Crockett, cannot be sustained based on other unquestioned identifications she made during the battle. As stated before, she had witnessed horrific scenes and was able to report them accurately.

Even more to the point, Mrs. Dickinson seeing Crockett's corpse in front of the Church is consistent with where Joe indicated he later identified Crockett for Santa Anna after the battle, and this also matches the description given by Almonte's cook, Ben. According to Ben, he was taken to the Alamo by Santa Anna and Almonte to further confirm Crockett's identity since he had previously seen David Crockett in person in a Washington, D.C., hotel. (Almonte had engaged Ben, a free person of color, as a servant/cook during his 1835 trip to the United States.) Dickinson's original identification of Crockett's body together with the corroborating statements by Joe, Ben, and Enrique Esparza is nearly irrefutable evidence of where Crockett died.

It is essential to grasp the absolute fact that in order for Dickinson (and also Esparza) to leave the Church and make her way to the Main Gate to exit the Alamo compound, she had to have gone out the front doorway of the Church and then through the gap opening in the Low Wall that stood 90 feet to the west of the Church. There simply was no other feasible exit out of the Church nor any other direct, unobstructed route out of the totally enclosed courtyard in front of the Church; Dickinson thus had to have walked right through the very area where she and all the rest of the eyewitnesses placed Crockett's dead body. (According to a number of their accounts, after being taken out of the Sacristy by Colonel Juan Almonte, the noncombatants were moved toward the front of the Church past the Confessional and temporarily held in the Church's Baptistry on the opposite side of the Nave [shown in Figure 1] for a brief interval before Almonte then led them to the outside of the Church.) (See Figures 1 and 2.)

(Here it is important that one additional point of evidence not go overlooked. Both Joe and Ben stated in particular [as did Dickinson and Esparza] that David Crockett lay completely surrounded by a large number of dead Mexican troops—a situation that would certainly not have been the case if Crockett had been lying at the site of the post-battle executions. [Joe even added the specific observation that "Colonel Crockett had the biggest pile."] Indeed, the statements by all four of these eyewitnesses [as well as a number of Mexican soldier accounts] explicitly describing Crockett being totally surrounded by slain Mexicans—if those statements are accurate and true—then that single fact alone demonstrates that Crockett could not have been one of the defenders who were executed [a prime example of strong circumstantial evidence].

This being the case, it must be emphasized that all four of these particular witnesses personally had the ability to recognize David Crockett and that all four of them made virtually identical statements about Crockett and the dead Mexican troops—those statements having been given independently by the individuals in separate interviews which took place in different locations and at different times. This particular element found in the testimony of all of these primary eyewitnesses actually constitutes a third evidentiary point that David Crockett was not executed that is independent of and in addition to the two others presented in this analysis.)

Enrique Esparza, another eyewitness and part of the same group that exited the Church along with Susannah Dickinson early that morning, stated that Crockett had fallen "immediately in front of the large double doors [the front doorway of the Church] which he defended with the force that was by his side. . . . There was a heap of slain in front and on each side of him." It was in front of the Church, at the South Palisade that Dr. John Sutherland tells us that Travis had assigned Crockett to defend on the first day of the siege, and that area is where Sutherland places his body on a map which he drew based on conversations with Joe.

We also have Henderson K. Yoakum's narrative that was published in 1855 that likewise tells us that Crockett was killed by the Church. Yoakum was a qualified historian, even by modern standards. His early history of Texas is easily the best researched and the single most important and consequential work on Texas's formative years. His sources, many of which he footnoted and others which have been lost, date back to the 1840's. Yoakum writes that Crockett was killed in a corner near the Church—with piles of slain around him. We do not know how he came upon that information or where he derived it from. But we do know that Susannah Dickinson was one of Yoakum's sources, and it is one more indication that David Crockett had died somewhere within the enclosed courtyard in front of the Church.

There is one other piece of testimony that needs to be factored into the Crockett death equation. Francisco Antonio Ruíz, the alcalde (mayor) of San Antonio de Béxar at the time, when asked by Santa Anna to be shown the body of Crockett, reported in a written statement which was published in the 1860 *Texas Almanac* that "toward the west, and in the small fort opposite the city, we found the body of Col. Crockett." From this, some battle students attempt to argue that Crockett's body was located at a cannon position protected by an exterior semicircular wooden palisade and earth fortification feature along the middle of the western wall.

The problem with this theory is that the best evidence—including the very accurate and meticulously detailed March 1836 pre-battle strategy map focusing specifically on the Alamo's defensive fortification features drawn up by Santa Anna's own chief engineer, Colonel Ygnacio de Labastida, and confirmed by modern-day archaeological investigations—indicates that no such feature existed anywhere on the western wall. Neither does the index nor the reconstructed plat from Alamo Engineer Green B. Jameson's report designate or depict any defensive feature of this nature at any point along the west wall. It was all just contiguous bare stone wall. Aside from the two gun platforms constructed at the northwest and southwest corners of the west wall, there were two cannon spaced out in between the corners at ground level, but these guns both fired through embrasures or openings in the wall and had no exterior (*nor interior*) protective works that could have appeared like a "small fort." None. (See Figure 2.)

That leaves only one remaining option. The feature Ruíz referred to as a "small fort" was almost undoubtedly the closed-off area in front of the Church, the so-called Inner Courtyard, which was enclosed by a "Low Wall" about 6 or 8 feet high some 90 feet in front of the Church on the west side, the 19-foot-high Long Barracks Connecting (or High) Wall on the north side, and the 7- to 8-foot-high wooden South Palisade (with sharpened points at the top of each post) on the south side—the area resembling a small fort since it was essentially walled off on all four sides—and "opposite the city" also fits because this enclosed area in front of the Church was situated almost directly opposite the downtown plazas of Béxar and was "toward the west" of the Church. The

Low Wall just referenced was also to the west of the Church. It is obvious that many witnesses of that era often used the Alamo Church in their accounts as their point of reference instead of the Alamo compound as a whole. In addition, there are numerous instances in the period accounts where it is clear that the Church and the "Alamo" in its entirety were being conflated.

There is also the confounding factor that the Ruíz account, after all, was a translation completed twenty-four years after the battle and his original written statement in Spanish has never been found. Consequently there is no notion as to what the actual descriptive phraseology or specific words were that Francisco Ruíz utilized, and it is well known by those who have dealt with Texas historical documents how notoriously inaccurate or at the very least misleading many if not most of these 19th-century translations from the Spanish to English can be, particularly if any Spanish idiomatic expressions or terms were involved. For example, depending on the exact words Ruíz used, instead of "toward the west," the phrase could have easily been more accurately translated as "facing toward the west," "facing the west," or "fronting the west."

Given all of the above, it is therefore well within the realm of possibility—even highly likely—that Ruíz is referring to the same location as Dickinson, Joe, Ben, and Enrique Esparza. The fact of the matter is that there simply *was* no other feature present at the Alamo on March 6, 1836 that would have resembled or could have conceivably been referred to as a "small fort." And furthermore, since all five of these eyewitnesses would have personally recognized David Crockett, it makes no logical sense that Ruíz would have described him as lying in an entirely different area of the compound than the other four. (One corollary observation that is worthy of note—even if somehow Crockett had been found killed inside of some small fortification feature on the western wall, that circumstance would still be in direct contradiction to the execution accounts.)

There is another important point connected to Francisco Ruíz on the subject of Crockett's identification that has never been brought to light before during this entire controversy. It turns out that a year after the publication of Ruíz's Crockett account, on April 16, 1861, Ruíz gave a deposition on behalf of the widow of Alamo defender Toribio Losoya swearing that he saw Losoya's dead body in the Alamo (he was among those killed inside the Church).

Of special relevance to the present investigation, Ruíz in this deposition also included the statement that "after the fall of the Alamo Gen. San Anna [*sic*] sent for affiant [Ruíz], *Don Ramón Músquiz and others* to identify the bodies of Travis, Bowie and Crockett *which was done* . . . . " (emphasis added). The deposition states nothing about who the "others" were, nor does it specify anything about any of the locations where the three leaders were found. However, it does not indicate that there was any disagreement or discrepancy with where Músquiz identified Crockett in relation to what Ruíz had stated. Since Ruíz and Músquiz were both personally acquainted with David Crockett it is a reasonable deduction that they both identified his body correctly and that they therefore both placed Crockett in the same location as that described by Ruíz. Santa Anna's ordering Ramón Músquiz in is highly significant given that for over two weeks prior to the siege—*David Crockett had been living in Músquiz's own house.*

The fact that Santa Anna would also bring in Músquiz further serves to bolster the contention that he (*and Almonte*) were by no means certain of the three Texans' identity—particularly with regard to Crockett. This is especially pertinent to the possible explanatory theory of events presented near the end of this analysis.

Considering the layout and structural perimeter of the Inner Courtyard as already described, this area would indeed appear like a small fort in front of—*and west of*—the Alamo Church. (See Figure 2.) Also perhaps germane to the matter of where Crockett died, it is readily apparent from the physical battle damage—impressions resulting from a multitude of artillery canister shot as well as hundreds of musket balls on the front face of the Church that is still clearly evident and visible to this day, especially that section of the Church face located north of the front door and extending all the way over to the northwest corner of the Church—that a ferocious last-stand conflict definitely did take place in this specific area.

(It should be mentioned here that there are some detractors who dispute the fact that Francisco Antonio Ruíz was even present in Béxar in March of 1836 at all, and that his accounts are therefore false. This contention is based solely on pure speculation—that "Ruíz would not have stayed around since Santa Anna was coming because his father was known to be an opponent of Santa Anna and had been sent as a delegate from Béxar to the General Convention in which the Texas Declaration of Independence was signed at Washington-on-the-Brazos on March 2." There is not one single scintilla of evidence whatsoever supporting such an assertion. On the contrary, as described above, Ruíz's sworn testimony regarding the Alamo was fully and officially accepted by the State of Texas, and the Losoya heirs received their land grants.)

There is yet a second critically important factor that is necessary to consider in regard to this subject— the specific locale of the events. At the time General Santa Anna entered the fort, the Mexican officers were reforming their battalions with the troops forming up by ranks—arrayed in a large hollow square according to Joe's description. Such a formation of necessity had to have been located out in the Main Plaza of the Alamo. Even after deducting battle casualties incurred that morning, these troops would have comprised well over one thousand men, probably around 1,200 or more. (And that is counting only that part of the infantry that had been committed to the actual assault. There were at least 700 additional troops—untrained recruits, musicians, cavalry, and artillerymen—who may or may not have been brought in after the battle to be present for Santa Anna's grand victory speech, bringing the potential total to almost two thousand men. Also pertinent to the timeline factor, it is known, according to de la Peña's account, that at least the *commander* of the cavalry which had been stationed outside the fort during the battle and had killed those attempting to flee, General Joaquín Ramírez y Sesma, was already present inside the Alamo by the time that the executions occurred.)

The walled-off enclosure or Inner Courtyard in front of the Church where all the primary eyewitnesses indicated they had seen Crockett's dead body would have been far too small (roughly 100 feet square or some 10,000 square feet) to have accommodated that large a number—anywhere within that range of 1,200 up to 2,000—of formally assembled troops. Physically and mathematically impossible.

The much more spacious Alamo Main Plaza (close to 85,000 square feet) therefore had to be the location

The Alamo by Andy Thomas, 2022 (Crockett's last stand)

where the troops were put into organized formation, where the executions took place, and directly thereafter where Santa Anna gave his victory speech to the army. This was the only area in the entire Alamo compound large enough to have held an organized force even half that size. Recall that earlier it was noted that according to the descriptions by both Ramón Caro and José Enrique de la Peña, the executions took place in the same location in which the Mexican troops were arrayed in formation by ranks. Consequently the executions had to have occurred in the Alamo's Main Plaza—not within the confines of the much smaller Inner Courtyard. If Crockett did in fact fall somewhere within that courtyard in front of the Church, it necessarily follows that he could not have died as a result of the executions that happened way out in the Alamo Main Plaza—an entirely different location. (See Figure 3.)

The issue regarding the actual location of the executions constitutes a second vital piece of evidence indicating that the Crockett execution story cannot be factual. And just as in the case of the timeline proof, it too has never previously been raised, presented, and analyzed. Because Susannah Dickinson and the rest of the eyewitnesses indicated that they saw David Crockett lying dead somewhere inside the enclosed courtyard in front of the Church (or in the Confessional room per Dickinson's later account), he therefore could not have been among those executed—and that holds true totally without regard to, and completely independent of, the crucial timeline proof that has already been presented herein.

In conducting this investigation, like any crime scene, the strongest evidence is usually the physical evidence—which in this case is the physical location of Crockett's dead body. In a case that is long after the fact like this one, that can only be determined by the testimony of the eyewitnesses to that location, and by determining the relative validity and weight of that testimony given by the witnesses. This procedure is known as Forensic Statement Analysis—a well-established and highly effective process employed in investigating cold cases through examination of the written record left by witnesses and weighing the best evidence from that testimony to reach a logical conclusion.

In the present case regarding David Crockett, as demonstrated elsewhere in this investigation, the relative validity of the witnesses and thus the weight of their testimony (at least *five* undeniably firsthand and identifiable eyewitness primary sources—all of whom would have recognized Crockett, versus *three* sources, at least two of which are of totally unknown identity—none of whom would have recognized Crockett) has to weigh heavily in favor of the location that is entirely inconsistent with Crockett being executed.

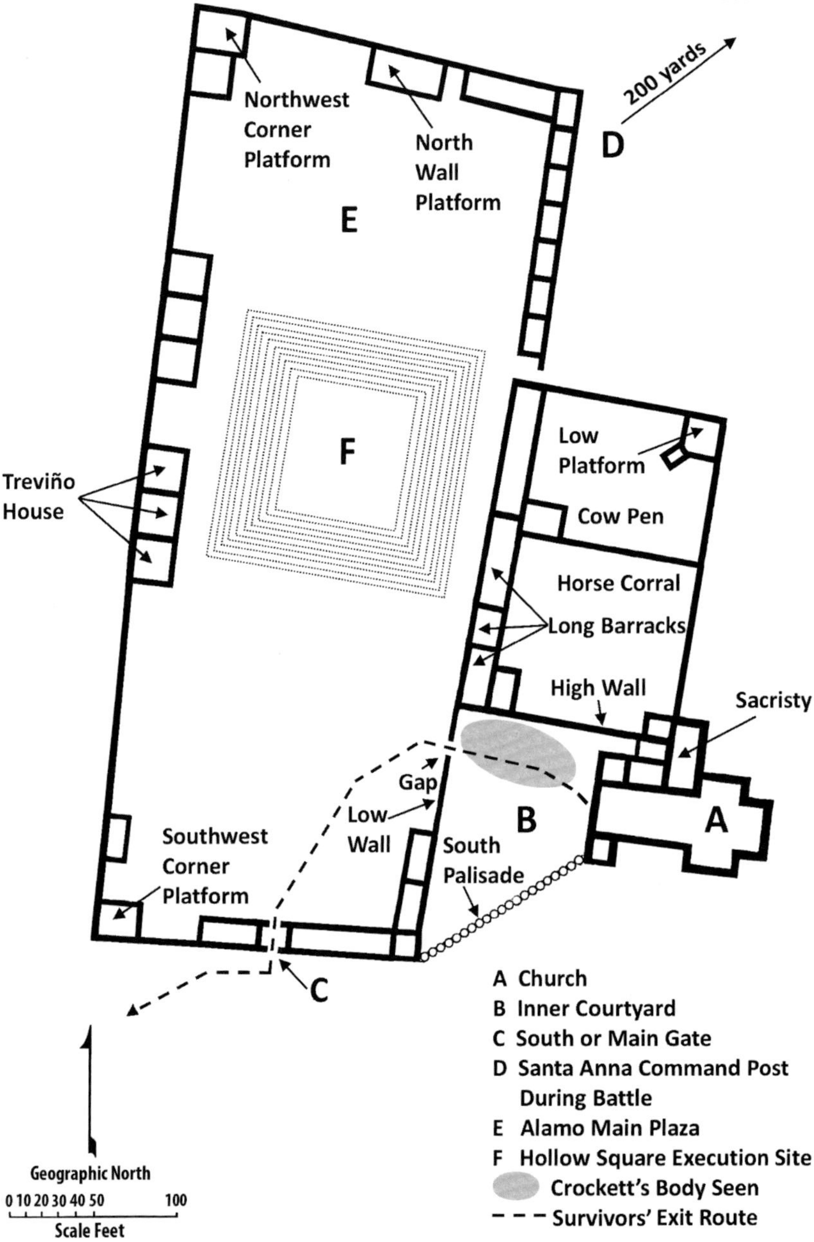

105

Figure 3. The entire Alamo compound showing the locations relating to the death of David Crockett and the site of the execution of the surviving Alamo defenders.

The relative strength of the extant evidence for each of the two sides of this controversy can essentially be boiled down to this:

The Crockett execution story is supported by nebulous, highly questionable, and often contradictory Mexican accounts that are frequently presented as definitive and overwhelming proof. These various narratives have the number of those executed ranging from only one all the way up to nine, and many of the accounts do not even mention or allude to Crockett at all, or at most do so very ambiguously. And that is not the full extent of their problems. Several are of completely unknown or questioned authorship; some are also second- and thirdhand accounts, thus constituting hearsay and double hearsay.

Even the much-vaunted, premier piece of evidence relied upon by the adherents of Crockett's execution, the de la Peña passage, cannot be considered a solid basis for the conclusion that Crockett was captured and executed. Even if Peña had been personally present as an eyewitness to the executions, there is still no reason to believe that he would have had the ability to recognize and identify David Crockett.

With regard to the hearsay problem concerning the Mexican accounts, the pre-eminent and most persuasive proponent of the Crockett execution theory (and along with Gregg Dimmick one of the most accomplished experts on the analysis of Mexican source documents),

Dr. James E. Crisp wrote in 2010 that the de la Peña account ". . . remains even today the *only* detailed description of Crockett's death composed by *an alleged eyewitness* . . . ." (emphasis added). Notably, Dr. Crisp also has written that Peña himself would not have had the ability to recognize David Crockett on sight.

In his excellent 2005 exegesis, *Sleuthing the Alamo*, Dr. Crisp directly addressed the problem of using the de la Peña account as a fundamental element of support for the Crockett execution story. After making a convincing argument that Peña himself was indeed the author of the manuscript and it is therefore authentic, a conclusion with which we fully agree, Crisp went on to state the following: "But as to *reliability*, the fact that de la Peña fashioned his longer narrative from multiple sources should make us cautious about accepting it as an authoritative account of how Davy died. Without corroboration from more reliable and immediate sources, de la Peña's story of the Alamo executions would have limited credibility."

Probably the most troubling aspect of all concerning the Peña account is the fact noted previously that it contains the same peculiar description of Crockett and the fabricated alibi statements allegedly made by Crockett that are quite obviously lifted straight out of the spurious story by Martín Perfecto de Cós that is universally acknowledged to be totally fraudulent and thoroughly discredited.

The fact of the matter is that all three of the main accounts that are regularly used to support Crockett's execution—the New York *Courier & Enquirer* article, the Dolson letter, and the account in the de la Peña diary—are not only in serious disagreement on multiple basic facts regarding the event, but most importantly, at least two of the three originate from sources *totally unknown and unidentified*. Indeed, upon close scrutiny and thorough examination, there exists not one single account or report coming directly from a *valid, identifiable* eyewitness known to have been *personally present* at the scene who would have been able to *recognize David Crockett on sight* that clearly and unambiguously identified Crockett as having been one of the defenders who were executed.

One point concerning the Mexican accounts of Crockett's execution serves to concentrate the focus down to a single factor that undermines the validity of them all. As discussed earlier, it is almost a certainty that the only member of the Mexican forces present at the Alamo following the March 6 battle who even *might* have had the ability to recognize David Crockett on sight was Colonel Juan N. Almonte; hence it was he alone who could have been the only possibly valid source who identified Crockett as being among the defenders executed. Even the major proponents of the Crockett execution story are in full agreement on this particular point.

The critical question then becomes: Did *Almonte* recognize Crockett on March 6, 1836? Upon close assessment, all the available evidence points to the conclusion that he did not.

It was previously stated herein that if Almonte had recognized Crockett, it is inconceivable that he would have failed to inform Santa Anna of David Crockett's identity prior to his execution. Even if that did actually occur, Almonte would have assuredly told Santa Anna after Crockett was dead, and if so, then why would Santa Anna have found it necessary to go to the trouble of ordering in at least six or more other individuals to go around and point out to him the body of Crockett. That simply makes no sense. It certainly does not indicate that Almonte had recognized Crockett, and as far as is known, Almonte never acknowledged having done so. In fact, it was Santa Anna *and Almonte* who subsequently went back to town and brought Almonte's cook, Ben, into the Alamo for the express purpose of identifying Crockett. That is yet another strong indication that Almonte had not recognized Crockett.

With Almonte being the only possible valid source regarding Crockett's execution, that then leaves only one remaining option. Some other Mexican thought (perhaps honestly) that one executed man who also could have been wearing buckskins was David Crockett and said so. As would be expected, the shocking tale then spread like wildfire. And once that rumor was out, it matters not whether there are five or fifty of these unnamed, anonymous sources later repeating the story; that still does not make it any more true. These subsequent accounts cannot be considered solid proof or even substantial evidence. In fact, evidentiary-wise, in a court of law they would all be thrown out as hearsay.

Referring specifically to such anonymous accounts as the Dolson letter and the *Courier & Enquirer* article, Alamo author Michael Lind aptly concluded that such hearsay evidence "appears extremely weak when compared to the eloquent silence on the subject of Crockett's execution in the accounts of the battle and its aftermath written by Almonte, Caro, Ruiz, and Santa Anna himself." Indeed, the silence on the part of all these major participants regarding any execution of David Crockett is not only eloquent—it is deafening.

In the final analysis, one fact ultimately renders any and all of the Mexican source accounts fatally flawed. There is no evidence nor any reason to believe that any person on the Mexican side present at the time of the executions on March 6, 1836—be they named or unnamed, identified or anonymous, truthful and sincere or purposely fraudulent—not one would definitely have had the ability to recognize and identify David Crockett on sight, and that very likely includes Juan Almonte.

In stark contrast to the sources supporting Crockett's execution, the following is true with regard to the five *primary* (all firsthand, not secondary) sources in opposition—Susannah Dickinson, Enrique Esparza, Francisco Ruíz, Travis's slave Joe, and Almonte's cook, Ben:

1. We know to a certainty *who* all of them were.
2. We know to a certainty that they were all *physically present* at the Alamo on March 6, 1836, and that they were all bona fide *eyewitnesses* to events that occurred there that day.
3. They all personally *knew* David Crockett (or had at least seen him in person in the case of Ben).
4. Their accounts all indicate that Crockett fell in the *same specific area* of the Fort—the enclosed courtyard in front of the Alamo Church.
5. Their accounts vary only as to the *exact spot* within the Church courtyard where Crockett fell—the sole exception being the one anomalous placement by Dickinson of Crockett lying inside the Church that was given very late in life but would still be in contradiction to the execution stories.

Each of the five points above are documented facts. Moreover, unlike many other Alamo sources, all five of these witnesses have been rated as strong and credible by Todd Hansen—arguably the foremost expert analyst of Alamo witness accounts.

The particular area where David Crockett lay is also a vital factor in the timeline proof since he would have had to have been at a site clearly visible to the two survivor eyewitnesses, Dickinson and Esparza, as they were being led out of the Alamo Church—again, certainly not the case if Crockett had been lying at some distant spot out in the Alamo Main Plaza where the executions occurred (and with visibility obscured by surrounding ranks of literally hundreds of assembled Mexican soldiers).

If *either* the execution location *or* the timeline sequence of events as have been previously demonstrated herein is accurate, then Crockett's execution becomes an impossibility. For both of these considerations—the execution-site disparity and the timeline proof—the determination of the correct *location* of Crockett's body is therefore the prerequisite fundamental basis necessary in reaching a final and accurate conclusion as to the circumstances of David Crockett's death.

In light of this fact, one important point remains to be emphasized. Enrique Esparza was the other key non-combatant survivor eyewitness who identified Crockett's body as he was being led out of the Church along with Susannah Dickinson. According to statements given in his various interviews, like Mrs. Dickinson, Esparza also had experienced extensive personal interactions with Crockett, especially throughout the twelve days of the siege during which time both of them were confined together inside the Alamo.

David Crockett obviously had made a stark impression on Enrique Esparza from the very first moment he entered the town with great fanfare on February 8, 1836:

> There was great cheering when Señor Crockett came with his friends. He wore a buckskin suit and a coonskin cap. He made everybody laugh and forget their worries. He had a gun he called "Betsey." They told me that he had killed many bears. I knew he would kill many of Santa Anna's soldiers.

Referring to the time they were together within the Alamo, Esparza stated the following: "He [Crockett] would often come to the fire and warm his hands and say a few words to us in the Mexican language." In a later interview Enrique had this to say:

> Señor Crockett seemed everywhere. He would shoot from the wall or through the portholes. Then he would run back and say something funny. He tried to speak Spanish sometimes. Now and then he would run to the fire we had in the courtyard where we were to make us laugh.

Similar episodes and encounters of this nature undoubtedly took place on a near-daily basis. Given the extent of all these close interactions, as was the case with Susannah Dickinson, Enrique Esparza clearly would have had no difficulty in recognizing David Crockett. And as Alamo witness analyst Todd Hansen emphasized, the shocking and gruesome sight of Crockett's bloody, mangled body would have undoubtedly left an indelible impression on the memory of someone even as young as eight years of age. In his evaluation of Enrique Esparza's testimony, Hansen stated, "Here again, the most vivid details are of events and situations that were likely to be stressful and therefore the most memorable." Hansen's final considered conclusion was that there is "overwhelming support for the validity of the Esparza story."

There is a possible scenario that could have transpired in which the various contradictory accounts and evidence might be explained in a way that they are mutually consistent and at least most (if not all) of the conflicts and contradictions reconciled—a credible, logical means of unwinding this seemingly unresolvable enigma by employing the method known as the dialectic or Hegelian process wherein the elements of two apparently opposite assertions are combined or merged in order to form a synthesis that constitutes the actual truth. This is of course totally speculative, but perhaps it is possible that something like the following occurred.

The execution event took place similar to the description contained in the Dolson letter. Almonte did initially think that the man in the rear was David Crockett and told the "informant," whoever that was, and for whatever reason did not or could not immediately alert Santa Anna—maybe because Santa Anna was too involved in lambasting Castrillón for not having already killed the prisoners. The rumor about Crockett's execution then subsequently got spread by the "informant" or someone else that *he* told and it took off from there.

Once the victim had been killed, Almonte may not have felt absolutely certain of his identity, or at least Almonte (and/or Santa Anna) wanted to verify that he was correct, and that is why Almonte and Santa Anna got several other people—first Joe, and then from the town Ben, Ruíz, Músquiz, and possibly others—to identify the body and Almonte turned out to be wrong. As identified by these bona fide witnesses (and matching the later accounts of Dickinson and Esparza), David Crockett's dead body was actually confirmed to be located up there somewhere inside the inner Church courtyard where he had fallen during the fighting.

This would also explain why Santa Anna writing his post-battle report at about 8:00 a.m. that morning shortly after the identifications had been made merely stated concerning Crockett that his body was among the corpses along with those of Travis and Bowie, and made no reference or claim bragging about Crockett being captured and executed. Also, why Crockett's execution was not mentioned in any of Santa Anna's subsequent writings nor in those of any of the other Mexican officers and officials who later wrote their own accounts—even in those that did mention the post-battle execution of Alamo defenders—Ramón Caro in particular.

If something similar to the series of events as described above did occur, that could account for all or most of the apparent discrepancies and contradictions in the accounts and in the evidence. This is clearly only a possible answer and is by no means a certainty, but it is a feasible explanation and one that is not impossible.

While many deconstructionists and iconoclasts have savored over the idea of Davy Crockett surrendering, even, as some would imaginatively have it, cringing and begging for his life (Carmen Perry gets so carried away in her deeply flawed translation that she has de la Peña referring to Crockett three times when he mentioned him only once in the original Spanish), nothing is more unsupported by the evidence. (And to be clear, unlike the radical revisionists, none of the *legitimate* historians who believe that Crockett was executed have expressed any such disparaging attitude whatsoever. Theirs has been an honest and sincere effort to determine the correct historical truth concerning Crockett's actual fate—not to demean Crockett's character or heroism in any way. We simply arrived at a different conclusion based on a full re-examination of all the evidence.) If anything, David Crockett seemed to have become more of a pawn or a weapon in a campaign orchestrated to sully Santa Anna and bring him to justice than he was an executed prisoner.

In the end, the answer to the whole controversy comes down to one common-sense question. Should not the sworn testimony of the people who actually knew the living, flesh and blood David Crockett and who personally saw with their own eyes his mangled mortal remains following right after the battle carry infinitely more weight than any number of rumors and tales which at their root originated almost totally from parties unknown and all of which did not even begin to be bandied about until a full six weeks following Crockett's death at the earliest? That question constitutes the real crux of this entire issue.

In consideration of that fact, Susannah Dickinson's original identification of Crockett's mutilated remains together with the corroborating statement by Enrique Esparza is very strong and prima facie evidence of where David Crockett died—in the enclosed courtyard area in front of the Church—and, most significantly, that his death had occurred before Santa Anna ever even entered the Alamo that morning and, hence, he could not have ordered the execution of someone already dead.

A COMPREHENSIVE ANALYSIS

In addition, because of physical and spatial realities, the location where all of the authentic eyewitnesses place David Crockett's body is utterly incompatible with and in direct contradiction to the site where the executions took place, and this determination constitutes yet another strong, highly probative element of evidence in the case against Crockett's execution—one that is totally irrespective and independent of the crucial timeline proof.

The upshot is that when one gathers all the facts regarding Crockett's death, as we have heretofore attempted, the preponderance of the evidence clearly demonstrates that whoever the executed prisoners were that morning of March 6, 1836, it is highly unlikely that any of them were Crockett.

On the contrary, the greatest likelihood—based upon all the evidence compiled herein—is that the famous frontiersman met a very different ultimate fate at the Alamo:

David Crockett went down fighting.

About the Bibliography

The English novelist William Makepeace Thackery said of the historian Thomas Babington Macaulay that he "reads twenty books to write a sentence; he travels a hundred miles to make a line of description." Thackery went on to justify this excess in that it gives the author perspective and analytical depth. And so it is that our research has been salted by an abundance of sources rather than to be caught wanting because of scarcity.

Admittedly, by no means do all of the sources listed herein touch directly on the subject of David Crockett nor of his death specifically, but they do furnish valuable background information on many of the aspects related to the matter. That being said, this is by definition a comprehensive rather than a selected bibliography.

It should also be noted that any personal accounts, letters, and other documents referenced in the text that are not separately listed in this bibliography are contained in *The Alamo Reader: A Study in History* by Todd Hansen which is included under "Books."

BIBLIOGRAPHY

PUBLISHED MATERIALS

BOOKS

Almonte, Juan N. *Almonte's Texas: Juan N. Almonte's 1834 Inspection, Secret Report, and Role in the 1836 Campaign.* Edited by Jack Jackson. Translated by John Wheat. Austin: Texas State Historical Association, 2003.

Baugh, Virgil E. *Rendezvous at the Alamo: Highlights in the Lives of Bowie, Crockett, and Travis.* Lincoln: University of Nebraska Press, 1960.

Becerra, Francisco. *A Mexican Sergeant's Recollections of the Alamo and San Jacinto.* Austin: Jenkins Publishing Company, 1980.

Borroel, Roger. *The Texan Revolution of 1836: A Concise Historical Perspective Based On Original Sources.* East Chicago, Ind.: La Villita Publications, 1989.

———. *Field Reports of the Mexican Army During the Texan War of 1836.* Vol. VI. East Chicago, Ind.: La Villita Publications, 2006.

Boyd, Bob. *The Texas Revolution: A Day-by-Day Account*. San Angelo, Texas: San Angelo Standard, Inc., 1986.

Brands, H. W. *Lone Star Nation: How a Ragged Army of Volunteers Won the Battle for Texas Independence—And Changed America*. New York: Doubleday, 2004.

Brear, Holly Beachley. *Inherit the Alamo: Myth and Ritual at an American Shrine*. Austin: University of Texas Press, 1995.

Burrough, Bryan, Chris Tomlinson, and Jason Stanford. *Forget The Alamo: the Rise and Fall of an American Myth*. New York: Penguin Press, 2021.

Cantrell, Gregg, and Elizabeth Hayes Turner, editors. *Lone Star Pasts: Memory and History in Texas*. College Station: Texas A&M University Press, 2007.

Caro, Ramón Martínez. *The Mexican Side of the Texan Revolution, by the Chief Mexican Participants*. Translated by Carlos Castañeda. Dallas: P. L. Turner Company, 1928.

Chabot, Frederick C. *The Alamo: Altar of Texas Liberty*. San Antonio: Naylor Publishing Company, 1931.

Chariton, Wallace O. *Forget the Alamo*. Plano, Tex.: Wordware Publishing, 1990.

———. *100 Days in Texas: The Alamo Letters*. Plano, Tex.: Wordware Publishing, 1990.

———. *Exploring The Alamo Legends*. Plano, Tex.: Wordware Publishing, 1992.

Chariton, Wallace O., Charlie Eckhardt, and Kevin R. Young. *Unsolved Texas Mysteries*. Plano, Tex.: Wordware Publishing, 1991.

Chemerka, William R. *The Alamo Almanac and Book of Lists*. Austin: Eakin Press, 1997.

———, editor. *Alamo Anthology: From the Pages of The Alamo Journal*. Austin: Eakin Press, 2005.

Corner, William. *San Antonio de Bexar: A Guide and History*. San Antonio: Bainbridge & Corner, 1890.

Crisp, James E. *Sleuthing the Alamo: Davy Crockett's Last Stand and Other Mysteries of the Texas Revolution*. New York: Oxford University Press, 2005.

Crockett, Davy. *An Autobiography of Davy Crockett*. Philadelphia: E. L. Carey and A. Hart. Boston: Allen & Ticknor, 1834.

Daughters of the Republic of Texas. *The Alamo Long Barrack Museum*. Dallas: Taylor Publishing Company, 1986.

Davis, John L. *San Antonio: A Historical Portrait*. Austin: Encino Press, 1978.

Davis, William C. *Three Roads to the Alamo: The Lives and Fortunes of David Crockett, James Bowie, and William Barret Travis*. New York: Harper-Collins Publishers, 1998.

———. *Lone Star Rising: The Revolutionary Birth of the Texas Republic.* College Station: Texas A&M University Press, 2006.

Day, James M., compiler. *The Texas Almanac 1856–1873: A Compendium of Texas History.* Waco, Tex.: The Texian Press, 1967.

DeShields, James T., editor. *Tall Men with Long Rifles: The Glamorous Story of the Texas Revolution, as Told by Captain Creed Taylor, Who Fought in That Heroic Struggle from Gonzales to San Jacinto.* San Antonio: Naylor Company, 1935.

Dimmick, Gregg J. *Sea of Mud: The Retreat of the Mexican Army After San Jacinto; An Archeological Investigation.* Austin: Texas State Historical Association, 2004.

Donovan, James. *The Blood of Heroes: The 13-Day Struggle for the Alamo—and the Sacrifice That Forged a Nation.* Little, Brown and Company, 2012.

Edmondson, J. R. *The Alamo Story: From Early History to Current Conflicts.* Lanham, Md.: Republic of Texas Press, 2000.

Fehrenbach, T. R. *Lone Star: A History of Texas and the Texans.* New York: MacMillian Publishing Company, 1968.

Filisola, Vicente. *Memoirs for the History of the War in Texas*. Translated by Wallace Woolsey. Austin: Eakin Press, 1987.

———. *General Vicente Filisola's Analysis of José Urrea's Military Diary: A Forgotten 1838 Publication by an Eyewitness to the Texas Revolution*. Edited by Gregg J. Dimmick. Translated by John R. Wheat. Austin: Texas State Historical Association, 2007.

Flores, Richard R. *Remembering the Alamo: Memory, Modernity, and the Master Symbol*. Austin: University of Texas Press, 2002.

Fox, Daniel E. *Traces of Texas History: Archeological Evidence of the Past 450 Years*. San Antonio: Corona Publishing Company, 1983.

Frazee, Steve. *The Alamo*. New York: Avon Book Division / Hearst Corporation, 1960.

Government of Great Britain. *Manuel of Field Fortification, Military Sketching, and Reconnaissance*. London: Printed under the Superintendence of Her Majesty's Stationery Office, 1871.

Government of Mexico. *A Manual for Military Posts; or a Treatise on Campaign Fortifications*. Written in French by Marshal Soult and translated to Spanish with notes and adjustments considered necessary for use by the military of the Republic of Mexico, by Citizen Manuel A. Cañedo, Colonel, Line Infantry and Commander of the regular army, Battalion of the State of Zacatecas. Mexico: Government Printing Office, 1825. The English translation from Spanish by Dora Guerra is on file at the Daughters of the Republic of Texas Library, San Antonio.

Groneman, Bill. *Heroes of the Alamo and Goliad*. San Antonio: Alamo Press, 1987.

———. *Alamo Defenders: A Genealogy; The People and Their Words*. Austin: Eakin Press, 1990.

———. *Defense of a Legend: Crockett and the de la Peña Diary*. Plano: Republic of Texas Press, 1994.

———. *Eyewitness to the Alamo*. Plano: Republic of Texas Press, 1996.

———. *Death of a Legend: The Myth and Mystery Surrounding the Death of Davy Crockett*. Taylor Trade Publishing, 1999.

———. *David Crockett: Hero of the Common Man*. Forge Books, 2005.

Habig, Marion A. *The Alamo Mission: San Antonio De Valero, 1718–1793*. Chicago: Franciscan Herald Press, 1977.

Haggard, J. Villasana. *Handbook for Translators of Spanish Historical Documents*. Austin: Archives Collections, The University of Texas, Photoprinted by Senco Color Press, Oklahoma City, 1941.

Haley, James L. *Texas: An Album of History*. Garden City, N.Y.: Doubleday and Company, 1985.

Hanighen, Frank C. *Santa Anna: The Naploeon of the West*. New York: Coward-McCann, Inc., 1934.

Hansen, Todd. *The Alamo Reader: A Study in History*. Mechanicsburg, Pa.: Stackpole Books, 2003. Personal accounts, letters, and other documents referenced in the text that are not separately listed in this Bibliography are contained in this source.

Hardin, Stephen L. *Texian Iliad: A Military History of the Texas Revolution, 1835–1836*. Austin: University of Texas Press, 1994.

———. *The Alamo 1836: Santa Anna's Texas Campaign*. Oxford: Osprey Publishing, 2001.

———, editor. *Houston Displayed, Or, Who Won the Battle of San Jacinto?* Dallas: The DeGolyer Library and William P. Clements Center for Southwest Studies, Southern Methodist University, 2020.

Hatch, Tom. *Encyclopedia of the Alamo and the Texas Revolution*. London: McFarland and Company, 1999.

Hauck, Richard Boyd. *Crockett: A Bio-Bibliography*. Westport, Conn.: Greenwood, 1982.

Haythornthwaite, Philip J. *The Alamo and the War of Texan Independence, 1835–1836*. Oxford: Osprey Publishing, 1986.

Heirs of Col. Crockett. *Davy Crockett's Almanack of Wild Sports in the West, Life in the Backwoods, & Sketches of Texas, 1837*. Nashville: Published by the heirs of Col. Crockett, 1837.

Herman, Marguerita Z. *Ramparts: Fortification from the Renaissance to West Point*. Garden City, N.Y.: Avery Publishing Group, 1992.

Holley, Mary Austin. *The Texas Diary, 1835–1838*. Edited by J. P. Bryan. Austin: University of Texas Press, 1965.

Houston, Andrew Jackson. *Texas Independence*. Houston: Anson Jones Press, 1938.

Hoyt, E. 1811. *Practical Instructions for Military Officers: Comprehending a Concise System of Military Geometry, Field Fortification and Tactics of Riflemen and Light Infantry*. Westport, Conn.: Greenwood Publishing Group, 1986.

BIBLIOGRAPHY

Hoyt, Edwin P. *The Alamo: An Illustrated History.* Dallas: Taylor Publishing Company, 1999.

Huffines, Alan C. *Blood of Noble Men: An Illustrated Chronology of the Alamo Siege and Battle.* Austin: Eakin Press, 1999.

———. *The Texas War of Independence, 1835–1836: From Outbreak to the Alamo to San Jacinto.* Oxford: Osprey Publishing, 2005.

Huneycutt, C. D. *The Alamo: An In-depth Study of the Battle.* New London, North Carolina: Gold Star Press, 1986.

Huthmacher, Ned Anthony. *One Domingo Morning: The Story of Alamo Joe.* New York: Vantage Press, 2004.

Ivey, James E. "Mission to Fortress: An Architectural History of the Alamo." Unpublished Manuscript.

Jackson, Jack. *Los Tejanos.* Stanford, Conn.: Fantagraphics Books, 1982.

Jackson, Ron. *Alamo Legacy: Alamo Descendants Remember the Alamo.* Austin: Eakin Press, 1997.

Jackson, Jr., Ron J. and Lee Spencer White. *Joe, The Slave Who Became An Alamo Legend.* Norman: University of Oklahoma Press, 2015.

Jenkins, John H. *The Papers of the Texas Revolution, 1835–1836.* 10 vols. Austin: Presidial Press, 1973.

Johnson, Frank W. *A History of Texas and Texans.* 5 vols. Chicago and New York: American Historical Society, 1914.

Kilgore, Dan. *How Did Davy Die?* College Station: Texas A&M University Press, 1978.

Kilgore, Dan and James E. Crisp. *How Did Davy Die? And Why Do We Care So Much?* College Station: Texas A&M University Press, 2010.

Kilmeade, Brian. *Sam Houston & the Alamo Avengers: The Texas Victory That Changed American History.* New York: Penguin Random House LLC, 2019.

Lindley, Thomas Ricks. *Alamo Traces: New Evidence and New Conclusions.* Lanham, Md.: Republic of Texas Press, 2003.

Lord, Walter. *A Time to Stand.* New York: Harper & Brothers, 1961.

Mahan, Dennis Hart. 1836. *A Complete Treatise on Field Fortification, With the General Outlines of the Principles Regulating the Arrangement, the Attack, and the Defense of Permanent Works.* New York: Greenwood Press, 1968.

Matovina, Timothy M. *The Alamo Remembered: Tejano Accounts and Perspectives.* Austin: University of Texas Press, 1995.

Maverick, Mary A. *Memoirs of Mary A. Maverick: A Journal of Early Texas.* Arranged by Mary A. Maverick and her son George Madison Maverick. Edited by Rena Maverick Green and Maverick Fairchild Fisher. San Antonio: Maverick Publishing Company, 2005.

McCaleb, Walter F. *The Alamo.* San Antonio: Naylor Company, 1961.

McKinney, Bobby J. *A Search for Texas: the Revolution–the Republic–the Relics, 1836–1846.* Rosenberg, Tex.: Mouth of Caney, 2006.

Montejano, David. *Anglos and Mexicans in the Making of Texas, 1836–1986.* Austin: University of Texas Press, 1987.

Moore, Stephen L. *Eighteen Minutes: The Battle of San Jacinto and the Texas Independence Campaign.* Dallas: Republic of Texas Press, 2004.

Myers, John Myers. *The Alamo.* Lincoln: University of Nebraska Press, 1948.

Navarro, José Antonio. *Defending Mexican Valor in Texas: José Antonio Navarro's Historical Writings, 1853–1857.* Edited by David R. McDonald and Timothy M. Matovina. Austin: State House Press, 1995.

Nelson, George S. *The Alamo: An Illustrated History.* San Antonio: Aldine Books, 1998.

Nevin, David. *The Texans.* New York: Time-Life Books, 1975.

Newell, Rev. Chester. *History of the Revolution in Texas, Particularly of the War of 1835 & '36.* New York: Wiley & Putnam, 1838.

Nofi, Albert A. *The Alamo and the Texas War for Independence.* Conshohocken, Pa.: Combined Books, Inc., 1992.

Pennypacker, Anna J. Hardwicke. *A History of Texas for Schools.* Austin: Mrs. Percy V. Pennypacker, 1924.

Peña, José Enrique de la. *La rebelión de Texas: manuscrito inédito de 1836 por un oficial de Santa Anna.* Edited by J. Sánchez Garza. Quoted portions translated by Richard L. Range. Mexico [City], 1955.

——— *With Santa Anna in Texas: A Personal Narrative of the Revolution.* Translated and edited by Carmen Perry. Quoted portions translated by Richard L. Range. Introduction by James E. Crisp. Expanded edition. College Station: Texas A&M University Press, 1975.

Petite, Mary Deborah. *1836 Facts about the Alamo and the Texas War for Independence.* New York: Da Capo Press, 1999.

Pohl, James W. *The Battle of San Jacinto.* Austin: Texas State Historical Association, 1989.

Potter, Reuben M. *The Fall of the Alamo: A Reminiscence of the Revolution of Texas.* San Antonio: Herald Steam Press, 1860.

Procter, Ben E. *The Battle of the Alamo.* Austin: Texas State Historical Association, 1986.

Ragsdale, Crystal Sasse. *Women & Children of the Alamo.* Austin: State House Press, 1994.

Reid, Stuart. *The Secret War for Texas.* College Station: Texas A&M University Press, 2007.

Roberts, Randy, and James S. Olson. *A Line in the Sand: The Alamo in Blood and Memory.* New York: Free Press, 2001.

Rosenthal, Phil, and Bill Groneman. *Roll Call at the Alamo.* Ft. Collins, Colo.: Old Army Press, 1985.

Sánchez Lamego, Miguel A. *The Siege & Taking of the Alamo.* Translated by Consuelo Velasco. Santa Fe, New Mexico: The Press of the Territorian, 1968.

Sánchez-Navarro, Carlos, editor. *La Guerra de Tejas: Memorias de un Soldado.* Mexico City: Editorial Polis, 1938.

San Jacinto Museum of History. *The Honor Roll of the Battle of San Jacinto: The Complete List of Participants and Personnel on Detached Services.* La Porte, Tex.: San Jacinto Museum of History Association, 1965.

Santa Anna, Antonio. Edited by Ann Fears Crawford. *The Eagle: The Autobiography of Santa Anna.* Kerrville, Tex.: State House Press, 1988.

Santos, Richard G. *Santa Anna's Campaign Against Texas, 1835–1836: Featuring the Field Commands Issued to Major General Vicente Filisola.* Waco: Texian Press, 1968.

Scheina, Robert L. *Santa Anna: A Curse upon Mexico.* Washington, D.C.: Brassey's, 2002.

Schoelwer, Susan Pendergast. *Alamo Images: Changing Perceptions of a Texas Experience.* Dallas: DeGolyer Library and Southern Methodist University Press, 1985.

Seguín, Juan N. *A Revolution Remembered: The Memoirs and Selected Correspondence of Juan N. Seguín.* Edited by Jesús F. de la Teja. Austin: State House Press, 1991.

Shackford, James A. *David Crockett: The Man and the Legend.* Chapel Hill: University of North Carolina Press, 1956.

Steen, Ralph W. *The Texas Story.* Austin: Steck-Vaughn, 1960.

Sutherland, John. *The Fall of the Alamo.* San Antonio: Naylor Press, 1936.

Thompson, Bob. *Born on a Mountaintop: On the Road with Davy Crockett and the Ghosts of the Wild Frontier.* New York: Crown, 2012.

Thompson, Frank. *The Alamo.* San Diego: Thunder Bay Press, 2002.

Tijerina, Andrés. *Tejanos and Texas Under the Mexican Flag, 1821–1836.* College Station: Texas A&M University Press, 1994.

Tinkle, Lon. *13 Days to Glory: The Siege of the Alamo.* New York: McGraw-Hill Book Company, Inc., 1958.

Todish, Tim J., and Terry S. *The Alamo Sourcebook, 1836: A Comprehensive Guide to the Alamo and the Texas Revolution.* Austin: Eakin Press, 1998.

Tolbert, Frank X. *The Day of San Jacinto.* New York: McGraw-Hill Book Company, Inc., 1959.

Tyler, Ron, Douglas E. Barnett, Roy R. Barkley, Penelope C. Anderson, and Mark F. Odintz. *The New Handbook of Texas.* Austin: Texas State Historical Association, 1996.

Uecker, Herbert G. *The Archaeology of the Alamo: A Self-Guided Walking Tour and Personal Account.* Bulverde, Tex.: Monte Comal Publications, 2001.

Wallace, J. Warner. *Cold-Case Christianity: A Homicide Detective Investigates the Claims of the Gospels.* Colorado Springs, Colo.: Published by David C. Cook, 2023.

Wallis, Michael. *David Crockett, The Lion of the West.* New York: W. W. Norton & Company, 2011.

Warren, Robert Penn. *Remember the Alamo!* New York: Random House, 1958.

Wheeler, J. B. *The Elements of Fortification for the Use of the Cadets of the United States Military Academy at West Point, N.Y.* New York: D. Van Nostrand, 1882.

Woodrick, James V. *Cannons of the Texas Revolution.* Austin: Self-Published, 2015.

Yoakum, Henderson. *A History of Texas from Its First Settlement in 1685 to Its Annexation to the United States in 1846.* 2 vols. New York: Redfield, 1855.

Zaboly, Gary S. *An Altar for Their Sons: The Alamo and the Texas Revolution in Contemporary Newspaper Accounts.* Buffalo Gap, Tex.: State House Press, 2011.

Zavala, Adina de. *The Story of the Siege and Fall of The Alamo.* San Antonio: Self-Published, 1911.

Zuber, William Physik. *My Eighty Years in Texas.* Austin: University of Texas Press. 1971.

ARTICLES

Covner, Craig R. "Before 1850: A New Look at the Alamo Through Art and Imagery." *The Alamo Journal* (November 1990).

Crisp, James E. "The Little Book That Wasn't There: The Myth and Mystery of the de la Peña Diary." *The Southwestern Historical Quarterly*, Vol. 98, No. 2 (October 1994).

———. "Documenting Davy's Death: The Problematic 'Dolson Letter' from Texas, 1836." *Journal of the West*, Vol. 46, No. 2 (Spring 2007).

Davis, William C. "How Davy Probably Didn't Die." *Journal of the Alamo Battlefield Association*, Vol. 2, No. 1 (Fall 1997).

Effler, Glenn A. "The Most Pathetic Days in Time: A Descriptive Account of the Final Days of the Alamo Siege (Part 2)." *The Alamo Dispatch*, No. 189 (Spring 2020).

Gracy, David B., II. "Just as I Have Written It: A Study of the Authenticity of the Manuscript of José Enrique de la Peña's Account of the Texas Campaign." *The Southwestern Historical Quarterly*, Vol. 105, No. 2 (October 2001).

Groneman, Bill. "Crockett's Last Stand." *Alamo Lore and Myth Organization*, Vol. 4, No. 4 (December 1982).

———. "Follow the Money." *The Alamo Journal*, No. 172 (August 2014).
Harburn, Todd. "The Crockett Death Controversy." *The Alamo Journal* (April 1991).
Harrigan, Stephen. "The Last Days of David Crockett." *American History* (April 2011).
Ivey, James E. "Southwest and Northwest Wall Gun Emplacements." *Alamo Lore and Myth Organization,* Vol. 3, No. 3 (September 1981).
———. "South Gate and its Defenses." *Alamo Lore and Myth Organization*, Vol. 3, No. 4 (December 1981).
———. "The Losoyas and The Texas Revolution." *Alamo Lore and Myth Organization,* Vol. 4, No. 1 (March 1982).
———. "Construction Methods Used at the Alamo." *Alamo Lore and Myth Organization*, Vol. 4, No. 2 (June 1982).
———. "Archaeological Evidence for the Defenses of the Alamo." *The Alamo Journal* (June 2000).
———. "Another Look at Storming the Alamo Walls." *The Alamo Journal* (March 2001).
———. "¡Viva la Patria es nuestro el Alamo! The Text and Translation of the José Juan Sánchez Navarro Narratives." *The Alamo Journal* (December 2001).

Jackson, Jack, and James E. Ivey. "Mystery Artist of the Alamo: José Juan Sánchez." *The Southwestern Historical Quarterly* (October 2001).

Lind, Michael. "The Death of David Crockett." *The Wilson Quarterly*, Vol. 22, No. 1 (Winter 1998).

Lindley, Thomas Ricks. "James Butler Bonham: October 17, 1835–March 6, 1836." *The Alamo Journal* (August 1988).

———. "Alamo Artillery: Number, Type, Caliber, and Concussion." *The Alamo Journal* (July 1992).

———. "William B. Travis: Father of the Texas Revolution." *The Alamo Journal* (March 2004).

Potter, Reuben M. "The Fall of the Alamo." *The Magazine of American History*, Vol. II, No. 1 (January 1878).

Steely, Skipper. "David Crockett's Visit to the Red River Valley." *East Texas Historical Journal*, Vol. 37, No. 1 (March 1999).

Taylor, Creed. "The Life of Creed Taylor." Louis Wiltz Kemp Papers, Center for American History, University of Texas at Austin.

Winters, James Washington. "An Account of the Battle of San Jacinto." *The Quarterly of the Texas State Historical Association* (July 1902-April 1903).

Zaboly, Gary S. "The Abatis." *The Alamo Journal* (December 2005).

JOURNALS

Alamo Dispatch
Alamo Journal
Alamo Lore and Myth Organization
East Texas Historical Journal
Journal of the Alamo Battlefield Association
Journal of the West
Quarterly of the Texas State Historical Association
Southwestern Historical Quarterly
Tennessee Historical Quarterly
Texas Almanac
Wilson Quarterly

MAGAZINES

American History
Magazine of American History
People
Texas Monthly
True West

NEWSPAPERS

Arkansas Gazette (Little Rock)
Dallas Morning News
Dallas Times Herald
Democratic Free Press (Detroit, Michigan)
Diario del Gobierno de la República Mexicana (Mexico City)
Houston Chronicle
Houston Post
Louisiana Advertiser (New Orleans)
Morning Courier and New-York Enquirer
Mississippi Free Trader and Natchez Gazette
National Intelligencer (Washington D.C.)
New-Orleans Commercial Bulletin
New Orleans Post and Union
New Philadelphia Times (Ohio)
New York Times
New Yorker
Philadelphia Pennsylvanian
Red River Herald (Natchitoches, Louisiana)
San Antonio Express
San Antonio Light
San Luis Advocate (Texas)
Telegraph and Texas Register
Wall Street Journal

ARCHIVAL COLLECTIONS

Archives Division, Texas General Land Office, Austin, Texas
Archives Division, Texas State Library, Austin, Texas
Archivo Historico Militar, Mexico City
Bexar County Clerk's Office, Spanish Archives of Bexar County, San Antonio, Texas
Center for American History, University of Texas at Austin
Daughters of the Republic of Texas Library, San Antonio, Texas
DeGolyer Library, Southern Methodist University, Dallas, Texas
Navy and Old Army Branch, Military Archives Division, National Archives, Washington, D. C.
San Antonio City Engineer's Office
Special Collections, Tulane University Library, New Orleans, Louisiana
United States Library of Congress, Washington, D.C.
United States Department of the Interior, National Parks Service, Washington, D.C.
University of California Bancroft Library, Berkeley

SELECTED DOCUMENTS

Alamo Artillery File. Vertical File, Daughters of the Republic of Texas Library, San Antonio, Texas.

Lieutenant Colonel Pedro de Ampudia. "Report on the consumption of munitions by the . . . [artillery] in its Batteries during the siege and the day of the assault on the . . . Fortress [of the Alamo]," March 21, 1836. Archivo Historico Militar, Expediente 1655:40, University of California Bancroft Library, Berkeley.

Lieutenant Colonel Pedro de Ampudia. "After-action report from the Commanding General of Artillery with regard to the occupation of Bejar and the taking of the Alamo," March 27, 1836. Archivo Historico Militar, XI / 481.3 / Expediente 1655, Mexico City.

The Tornel Decree, December 30, 1835. *The Mexican Side of the Texan Revolution, by the Chief Mexican Participants*. Translated by Carlos Casteñada. Dallas: P. L. Turner Company, 1928.

"San Luís Battalion Daily Log." José Enrique de la Peña Papers, Center for American History, University of Texas at Austin.

Description of Mission San Antonio de Valero, October 15, 1727 by Fray Miguel Sevillano de Paredes. Provided courtesy of James E. Ivey.

Report on Mission San Antonio de Valero, June 5, 1745 by Fray Francisco Ortiz. Provided courtesy of James E. Ivey.

Report on Mission San Antonio de Valero, June 9, 1756 by Fray Francisco Ortiz. Provided courtesy of James E. Ivey.

Report on Mission San Antonio de Valero, April 25, 1759 by Fray Dolores y Biana. Provided courtesy of James E. Ivey.

Description of Mission San Antonio de Valero, March 6, 1762 by Fray Dolores y Biana. Provided courtesy of James E. Ivey.

Inventory of Mission San Antonio de Valero, December 14, 1772 by Fray Juan José Saenz de Gumiel. Provided courtesy of Craig R. Covner.

Diary and Report on Mission San Antonio de Valero, February 9, 1778 by Fray Juan Augustín de Morfi. Provided courtesy of James E. Ivey.

Description of Mission San Antonio de Valero, May 5, 1786 by Fray José Francisco López. Provided courtesy of James E. Ivey.

Inventory of Mission San Antonio de Valero at the Time of Secularization, April 23, 1793 by Fray José Francisco López. Provided courtesy of Martha Doty Freeman.

BIBLIOGRAPHY 151

Property grant to Pedro de los Angeles Charlí by
Fray Joseph Francisco López, May 25, 1786.
Bexar County Clerk's Office, Spanish Archives
of Bexar County, San Antonio, Texas.

Order of possession to Doña María Estrada (widow
of Pedro de los Angeles Charlí) by Don Manuel
Muñoz, April 25, 1793. Bexar County Clerk's
Office, Spanish Archives of Bexar County,
San Antonio, Texas.

Survey for property grant to Alexandro Treviño,
April 28, 1829. Bexar County Clerk's Office,
Spanish Archives of Bexar County, San Antonio,
Texas.

Articles of agreement between Gregorio Soto and Peter
Pauly concerning mason work on the former
Treviño house, March 10, 1856. Bexar County
Clerk's Office, Spanish Archives of Bexar County,
San Antonio, Texas.

François Giraud, City Surveyor. "Plat and Field Notes
. . . surveyed for S. A. Maverick," December 1849.
Book 1, San Antonio City Engineer's Office.

Deed of sale by Carmel de los Reyes to Samuel A.
Maverick, February 24, 1850. Bexar County
Clerk's Office, Spanish Archives of Bexar County,
San Antonio, Texas.

Deed for sale of the Galera (the "Low Barracks") by the Roman Catholic Church to the City of San Antonio, with survey by C. Hartnett, Surveyor and Engineer of the City of San Antonio, June 1, 1871. Bexar County Clerk's Office, Spanish Archives of Bexar County, San Antonio, Texas.

Historic American Buildings Survey, Mission San Antonio de Valero, August, 1961. United States Department of the Interior, National Parks Service, Library of Congress, Washington, D.C.

"Journal of Samuel Augustus Maverick." Maverick Family Papers, 1660–1938, Center for American History, University of Texas at Austin.

Minutes of Nacogdoches Meeting, March 26, 1836. Archives Division, Texas State Library, Austin.

Deposition by Francisco Antonio Ruíz, April 16, 1861 for the heirs of Toribio Losoya. Archives Division, Texas General Land Office, Austin.

"Testimony of Mrs. Hannig [Susannah Dickinson] touching the Alamo Massacre," September 23, 1876. Archives Division, Texas State Library, Austin.

LETTERS

Green B. Jameson to Samuel Houston, January 18, 1836.

William B. Travis to the People of Texas and all Americans in the world, February 24, 1836.

William B. Travis to Samuel Houston, February 25, 1836.

Robert M. Williamson to William B. Travis, March 1, 1836.

Antonio López de Santa Anna to José María Tornel, March 6, 1836.

Samuel Houston to James W. Fannin, March 11, 1836.

ARCHAEOLOGICAL DATA

Center for Archaeological Research, University of Texas at San Antonio

Earth Measurement Corporation, Cypress, Texas

South Texas Archaeological Research Services, LLC, San Antonio, Texas

Southern Texas Archaeological Association, San Antonio, Texas

ARCHAEOLOGICAL REPORTS

Eaton, Jack D. *Excavations at the Alamo Shrine (Mission San Antonio de Valero).* Special Report No. 10, Center for Archaeological Research, University of Texas at San Antonio, 1980.

Fox, Anne A., Feris A. Bass, Jr., and Thomas R. Hester. *The Archaeology and History of Alamo Plaza.* Archaeological Survey Report No. 16, Center for Archaeological Research, University of Texas at San Antonio, 1976.

Fox, Anne A., and James E. Ivey. *Historical Survey of the Lands Within the Alamo Plaza—River Linkage Development Project.* Archaeological Survey Report No. 77, Center for Archaeological Research, University of Texas at San Antonio, 1979.

Fox, Anne A. *Archaeological Investigations in Alamo Plaza, San Antonio, Bexar County, Texas, 1988 and 1989.* Archaeological Survey Report No. 205, Center for Archaeological Research, University of Texas at San Antonio, 1992.

Hard, Robert J., editor. *A Historical Overview of Alamo Plaza and Camposanto.* Special Report No. 20, Center for Archaeological Research, University of Texas at San Antonio, 1994.

Ivey, James E. "Mission to Fortress: The Defenses of the Alamo." Unpublished Manuscript, Center for Archaeological Research, University of Texas at San Antonio.

Meissner, Barbara A. *The Alamo Restoration and Conservation Project*. Archaeological Survey Report No. 245, Center for Archaeological Research, University of Texas at San Antonio, 1996.

OTHER SOURCES

Edward Aranda: San Antonio, Texas, researcher of property deed records from 19th-century San Antonio.

Joe M. Austin: Houston, Texas, Professional Geoscientist and Owner of Earth Measurement Corporation.

Alwyn Barr: Lubbock, Texas, Professor of History, Texas Tech University; Texas Revolution scholar and author.

Mel Brown: Austin, Texas, fourth-generation San Antonian; Texas historian and artist.

Hector J. Cardenas: San Antonio, Texas, one of the original founders and President of the Friends of San Pedro Springs Park.

William R. Chemerka: Barnegat, New Jersey, Founder, The Alamo Society; Publisher and Editor of *The Alamo Journal* from 1986 to 2014; Alamo historian, author, and educator.

Craig R. Covner: San Diego, California, Alamo architectural historian and artist.

Carolyn Cotton: Clifton, Texas, great-great-great-granddaughter of David Crockett.

James E. Crisp: Raleigh, North Carolina, Associate Professor of History, North Carolina State University; Texas Revolution scholar and author.

Jan DeVault: Houston, Texas, President, The San Jacinto Battleground Conservancy.

Ellen Maverick Dickson: San Antonio, Texas, great-granddaughter of Samuel Augustus Maverick.

Gregg J. Dimmick, M.D.: Wharton, Texas, Texas Revolution historian, author, and archaeologist.

James Donovan: Dallas, Texas, Alamo historian and author.

Ed Dubravsky: York, Maine, Alamo researcher and small arms expert.

Jeffrey D. Dunn: Dallas, Texas, Chairman, San Jacinto Historical Advisory Board; Vice-President, The San Jacinto Battleground Conservancy; and former Chairman, Dallas County Historical Commission.

David A. Esparza: Schertz, Texas, great-great-grandson of Alamo defender José Gregorio Esparza.

Tom Feely: Jackson, Pennsylvania, Alamo historian and diorama artist.

Lewis F. Fisher: San Antonio, Texas, San Antonio historic building preservation historian and author.

Garon Foster: San Antonio, Texas, Forensic Scientist, Bexar County Criminal Investigation Laboratory.

Anne A. Fox: Alamo archaeologist and Humanities Research Associate, Center for Archaeological Research, University of Texas at San Antonio.

Harold D. Fulton: Cypress, Texas, Professional Geoscientist.

Bill Groneman: Kerrville, Texas, Alamo historian, author, and noted authority on the Alamo defenders; Publisher and Editor of *The Alamo Journal* from 2014 to 2017.

Kenneth Hafertepe: Waco, Texas, Associate Professor of Museum Studies, Baylor University.

Todd Hansen: Tucson, Arizona, Alamo author, researcher, and historian.

Mike Harris: Lenapah, Oklahoma, Alamo researcher, historian, and model artist.

Evan Hocker: Archivist, Center for American History, University of Texas at Austin.

Lieutenant Colonel Alan C. Huffines, U.S. Army: Abilene, Texas, Alamo historian, author, and military expert.

James E. Ivey: Santa Fe, New Mexico, Historical Archaeologist, National Park Service, Southwest Regional Office; authority on Alamo archaeology and architecture.

Jack Jackson: Austin, Texas, early Texas cartography expert, historian, and author.

Patrick Lemelle: San Antonio, Texas, Library Program Coordinator, Institute of Texan Cultures.

Patsy Pittman Light: San Antonio, Texas, Béxar and Goliad researcher and historian.

Thomas Ricks Lindley: Nixon, Texas, Alamo historian and author; expert on Alamo artillery.

Stephanie Malmros: Head of Archives and Manuscripts, Center for American History, University of Texas at Austin.

Terrellita Maverick: San Antonio, Texas, great-granddaughter of Samuel Augustus Maverick.

Bobby J. McKinney: Rosenberg, Texas, Member, Fort Bend County Historical Commission; Texas Revolution historian, author, and archaeologist.

Bruce K. Moses: San Antonio, Texas, Chairman, Southern Texas Archaeological Association; Research Associate, Center for Archaeological Research, University of Texas at San Antonio.

George S. Nelson: Uvalde, Texas, Alamo historian, author, and artist.

Samuel P. Nesmith: San Antonio, Texas, Director, Texas Museum of Military History and former Curator of the Alamo; military historian, author, and collector.

Cheryl B. Nesmith: San Antonio, Texas, Secretary, Texas Museum of Military History; military historian and collector.

Bradley L. Ponder: San Antonio, Texas, Alamo researcher and historian.

John B. Richardson: San Antonio, Texas, Senior History Interpreter, History Department, The Alamo.

Alfred Rodriguez: San Antonio, Texas, former Bexar County Spanish Archivist.

George P. Rollow: Austin, Texas, Colonel of Artillery, Texas Army, Texas Living History re-enactor and authority on 19th-century small arms and artillery.

Margaret Schlankey: Head of Public Services, Center for American History, University of Texas at Austin.

Kenny Schneider: Canyon, Texas, Exhibits Construction Manager, Panhandle-Plains Historical Museum.

Albert Seguin Gonzalez: Texas City, Texas, great-great-great-grandson of Juan Nepomuceno Seguín.

William R. Simmons: Austin, Texas, Research Assistant, Texas State Library and Archives Commission.

Elizabeth B. Standifird: San Antonio, Texas, Librarian, San Antonio Conservation Society.

Randell Tarin: Tyler, Texas, great-great-great-grandson of Vicente Tarín, early 19th-century commandant of The Second Flying Company of Alamo de Parras.

Dr. Steve A. Tomka: former Director, Center for Archaeological Research, University of Texas at San Antonio.

Ed Townes: Fort Worth, Texas, Professor of Southwestern U.S. History, Texas Christian University.

Annette Losoya Tynan: San Antonio, Texas, fifth-generation grandniece of Alamo defender José Toribio Losoya.

Herbert G. Uecker: Bulverde, Texas, Cultural Resources Director and Principal Investigator, South Texas Archaeological Research Services, LLC; Alamo archaeologist, author, and artist.

Martha Utterback: San Antonio, Texas, Assistant Director, Daughters of the Republic of Texas Library, San Antonio.

Janet K. Wagner: Houston, Texas, archival researcher.

Reuben Maverick Welsh, Jr.: Corpus Christi, Texas, great-great-grandson of Samuel Augustus Maverick.

Lee Spencer White: Fredericksburg, Texas, Alamo Defenders Descendants Association and fifth great-granddaughter of Gordon C. Jennings, oldest known defender at the Alamo

Gary R. Wiggins: Highlands, Texas, San Jacinto native, historian, author, and archaeologist.

James V. Woodrick: Austin, Texas, Texas Revolution artillery researcher, author, and historian.

Charles M. Yates: Austin, Texas, Texas Living History re-enactor and authority on 19th-century small arms and artillery.

Gary S. Zaboly: Riverdale, New York, Alamo artist and historian.

Richard Range—*A long, long time ago, in a place far, far away—me and the old bygone Texas as we once were—and never to be again. (Llano County, Texas—circa 1968)*